WAYWARD YOUTH

WAYWARD YOUTH

BY

AUGUST AICHHORN

WITH A FOREWORD BY

SIGMUND FREUD

NORTHWESTERN UNIVERSITY PRESS

VERWAHRLOSTE JUGEND
First published 1925 by INTERNATIONALER PSYCHOANALYTISCHER VERLAG,
Vienna   All rights reserved   Second Edition 1931

WAYWARD YOUTH
Revised and adapted from the second German edition
Copyright 1935, Renewed 1963 by THE VIKING PRESS, INC.

NORTHWESTERN UNIVERSITY PRESS PAPERBACK edition
First printing 1983

Printed in the United States

FOREWORD
By Sigmund Freud

Of all the fields in which psychoanalysis has been applied none has aroused so much interest, inspired so much hope, and accordingly attracted so many capable workers as the theory and practice of child training. This is easy to understand. The child has become the main object of psychoanalytic research and in this respect has replaced the neurotic with whom the work began. Analysis has revealed that the child lives on almost unchanged in the sick patient as well as in the dreamer and the artist; it has thrown a flood of light on the instinctual forces and impulses which give the childish being its characteristic features; and it has traced the paths of development which proceed to maturity. It is no wonder that expectation was aroused that psychoanalytic work would prove valuable in education, the purpose of which is to guide the child on his way to maturity, to encourage him, and to protect him from taking the wrong path.

My personal share in this application of psychoanalysis has been slight. In my youth, I accepted it as a byword that the three impossible professions are teaching, healing, and governing, and I have been sufficiently busy with the second. This does not mean that I do not appreciate the great social value of the work which attracts my co-workers in the pedagogical field.

August Aichhorn's book deals with one part of the great problem of the application of psychoanalysis to education, namely, that of influencing the dissocial adolescent by means of education. The author had worked for many years in an official position as director of state institutions for the care of delinquents before he became acquainted with psychoanalysis. His treatment of his charges had its source in a warm sympathy for the fate of these unfortunates and was rightly guided by his intuitive understanding of their psychic needs. Psychoanalysis could teach him little that was new to him in a practical way, but it offered him a clear theoretical insight into the justification of his treatment and enabled him to explain his method to others in this field.

We cannot assume that every educator has this intuitive gift. Aichhorn's experience and achievement lead us to two conclusions. One is that the educator should be psychoanalytically trained; otherwise the child, the object of his effort, remains an inaccessible enigma to him. Such training is best achieved when the educator subjects himself to an analysis in order to experience it within himself. Theoretical teaching of analysis does not penetrate deeply enough and brings no conviction.

The second conclusion sounds rather more conservative in its purport, that educational work is *sui generis*, not to be confused with nor exchanged for psychoanalytic means of influence. Psychoanalysis of the child may be drawn upon as a contributory help, but it is not an appropriate substitute for education. This is true not only because of

practical reasons, but also because of theoretical considerations. The relation between education and psychoanalytic
work will probably be the subject for a detailed investigation in the near future. I shall indicate only a few points
here. One must not be led astray by the statement, quite
justified in another sense, that psychoanalysis of the adult
neurotic may be compared to re-education. The child, even
the wayward and delinquent child, should not be compared
to the adult neurotic, and re-education is something quite
different from the education of the immature. The possibility of exerting influence through psychoanalysis depends
on quite definite conditions, which may be described as the
"analytic situation"; it requires the formation of certain
psychic structures and a special attitude toward the analyst. When these factors are lacking, as in the case of
children and young delinquents and, as a rule, in criminals
dominated by their instincts, the psychoanalytic method
must be adapted to meet the need. The theoretical chapters
of this book offer the reader a preliminary orientation in
these various considerations.

I add one more conclusion, which has no special significance for the theory of pedagogy but is important for the
position of the educator. If a teacher has learned analysis
by experiencing it himself and is capable of applying his
knowledge as a supplementary aid in his work with border-
line and mixed cases, he should obviously be allowed the
practice of analysis and should not be hindered in it for
narrow-minded reasons.

CONTENTS

WAYWARD YOUTH

ONE

INTRODUCTION

In the following pages I propose to discuss the application of psychoanalysis to the treatment of delinquent youth. This presentation offers an orientation in the subject rather than any final word. I shall give examples from my own experience together with pertinent theoretical considerations but I should warn beginners in this field that I can lay down no hard and fast rules of procedure. My intention is to arouse thoughtful consideration of the problems discussed and to stimulate independent effort.

I assume that psychoanalysis is familiar to you as a method of treatment for certain nervous disorders, primarily the neuroses. This book will take up the application of psychoanalysis to a special branch of pedagogy and will show how it can give the worker with problem children the psychological understanding requisite for his task. Psychoanalysis enables the worker to recognize dissocial manifestations as the result of an interplay of psychic forces, to discover the unconscious motives of such behaviour, and to find means of leading the dissocial back to social conformity.

By "wayward youth" I do not mean merely delinquent and dissocial children but also so-called problem children and others suffering from neurotic symptoms. A strict defi-

3

nition or delimitation of these groups is difficult because they tend to merge into each other. You are familiar with these cases from everyday observation, in social work, in the child-guidance clinic, in the Juvenile Court, and in similar contacts.

At the outset, it is important that we learn to differentiate the phases of dissocial behaviour. Every child is at first an asocial being in that he demands direct primitive instinctual satisfaction without regard for the world around him. This behaviour, normal for the young child, is considered asocial or dissocial in the adult. The task of upbringing is to lead the child from this asocial to a social state. But this training cannot be successful unless the libidinal development of the child pursues a normal course. Given certain disturbances in the libido organization, the nature of which cannot be discussed here, the child remains asocial or else behaves as if he had become social without having made an actual adjustment to the demands of society. This means that he has not repudiated completely his instinctual wishes but has suppressed them so that they lurk in the background awaiting an opportunity to break through to satisfaction. This state we call "latent delinquency"; it can become "manifest" on provocation. The change from latent to manifest delinquency usually occurs gradually during a period in which no definite symptoms are to be seen, but in which "susceptibility" can already be perceived. Observant parents recognize that the child in this state is endangered, and seek help in the guidance clinic. The child brought to us in this phase of susceptibility offers the best prognosis for treatment. However, during the treatment in this period, we must be prepared for surprises; for example, a symptom may suddenly disappear. The beginner in this field is often deceived by this, thinking that he has achieved a cure. But the disappearance of the symptom may indicate only a return to the former latent condition. The instinctual wishes may have been suppressed because of the child's attachment to the worker or because of some anxiety or fear which is not recognized. Our work is finally successful when a recurrence is made impossible, that is, when the suppression of instinctual wishes is transformed into an actual renunciation of these wishes through the laying bare of unconscious relationships.

The treatment of the delinquent is a matter of reeducation. Before we take up this special aspect of training and the application of psychoanalytic principles, let us consider the purpose of education in general. There are two fundamental points of view. One opinion is that a child's development is determined by heredity alone and cannot be changed by education; the other, that education can achieve any desired end and can overcome even hereditary difficulties. Before we subscribe to either attitude, let us consider the history of human development. The first task of early man was to develop a certain primitive capacity to cope with reality in order to escape annihilation. What does this mean in psychic development? The human being has had to learn to endure pain, to postpone and renounce satisfaction, and to divert primitive instinctual urges into socially acceptable channels. Thus through the centuries a civilization has developed within which man, with his technical achievements, strides steadily forward conquering nature and continuously creating artistic, scientific, and social works.

From this it follows that the lower or primitive cultural level is characterized by less restriction of immediate satisfaction of instinctual drives, and that the original primitive capacity to cope with reality increases with cultural development. This heightened capacity to cope with reality we regard as the capacity of the individual to share in the general culture of his age, and this we term culture-capacity. This may be assumed to vary quantitatively, according to the cultural level achieved. The original primitive reality-capacity remains as a constant. How is this to be understood? Leaving this question for the present, let us consider the child in the course of his development. The younger he is, the less he is able to deny himself the fulfilment of his instinctual wishes and to conform to the requirements of social life. Only under the pressure of painful experience does he gradually learn to impose restrictions upon his impulses and to accept the demands of society without conflict, and thus becomes social. The path which the child must traverse from the unreal pleasure-world of his nursing period to the real world of the adult, parallels that of mankind from primitive times to the present. It may be longer or shorter according to the particular cultural level, but must be traversed by the child in those few years during which he ripens to maturity. As with the physical development of the immature organism, this may be regarded as the ontogenetic repetition of phylogeneti-cally determined change. Although the new-born child brings with him traces of the accumulated experience of his ancestors, this endowment is not sufficient equipment for adjustment to the society in which he finds himself. His inherent capacity must be expanded through education and experience.

Thus man becomes civilized through experience and training. Life forces him to conform to reality; education enables him to achieve culture. This we observe in everyday life. A child who climbs on a chair, falls, and hurts himself learns caution directly through pain, without any outer intervention. This tendency toward self-preservation leads the child toward further social conformity. To the child who lacks the constitutional endowment necessary for primary adaptation to reality, education has little to offer. Education is no more than a means for unfolding existing potentialities and cannot add anything new to the individual. The child who grows up without appropriate training does not fit into the social order and therefore comes into conflict with society.

We see this demonstrated in the delinquent child. Our work as remedial educators begins when an educational emergency arises, that is, when the usual educational methods have not succeeded in developing in the child or youth the social capacity normal for his age level. In purpose, our initial work does not differ from education in general, since both attempt to fit the child for his place in society. Therefore we shall concern ourselves primarily

with method, the application of psychoanalytic principles
to the problems involved.

Psychoanalysis was developed by Sigmund Freud in his
treatment of neurotic patients. He demonstrated that emotion blocked in its direct outlet seeks discharge over a
devious pathway. Means of overt discharge are various,
following the line of least resistance. For instance, one
person may discharge emotion through secretory activity,
as in weeping; another through motor activity as in scolding, hitting, and the like, and still another through vaso-
motor responses, as in blushing. For civilized man, some of
these motor responses are not permissible and the affective
situation must be repressed, that is, it must be pushed back
from consciousness into the unconscious whence it seeks
expression in a disguised form. This same force which excludes inadmissible material from consciousness prevents
the repressed material from becoming conscious. This we
call "resistance." Other factors may operate to cause repression, for example, a traumatic experience in which the
degree of emotion is too great for assimilation. We shall
discover how dissocial behaviour can be an outlet for repressed emotion.

The assumption of the unconscious has provoked many
objections. However, as Freud deepened his researches into
the unconscious mental life, it became clear to him that
all mental processes are interrelated. Every mental event
and every given psychic situation are the result of the interplay of psychic forces. This dynamic conception is basic
in our understanding of the way unconscious mechanisms

determine behaviour. It becomes possible for the remedial educator to discover the motivation of delinquency and thus to obtain a point of attack for treatment. A situation becomes clear to the educator only when he knows the dynamic forces which produced it. His task is to bring into consciousness those unconscious processes which determine the undesirable behaviour. It should be clearly understood that neither the delinquent nor the neurotic individual has any conscious realization of the relation between his behaviour and its deeper causation. The educator will be better able to grasp the difficulties of his charge when he understands more completely his own mental processes. This understanding will be increased if he himself is psychoanalyzed.

Symptoms of delinquency can arise from a neurotic basis. When the neurotic factors predominate, the usual educational methods are therapeutically inadequate. In such cases, psychoanalytic understanding of neurosis offers the most effective contribution to our work. When symptoms of delinquency are not predominantly neurotically determined, pedagogical skill is important because of the necessity to regulate the child's environment. It might appear superfluous to stress the important role of the educator in this field were it not that there appears to be a tendency to reserve this field as the domain of the physician. In every case, the educator should consult a psychoanalytically trained physician so that disease will not be overlooked.

Although psychoanalysis has made an inestimable contribution to the understanding of the underlying motives of behaviour, we must not overlook the fact that remedial education accomplished many good results before we had any psychoanalytic insight. Educational work is an art, in which intuition is of primary importance. This holds true in greater measure for remedial training than for general education. The more intuitively the worker grasps the difficulties of his charge, the more successfully he works. It must be granted that technical skill derived from a definite knowledge of the normal predictable course of mental processes enhances the efficacy of his work. When the psychic mechanisms revealed by psychoanalysis are familiar to the educator, what has been intuitive understanding becomes a conscious recognition of the forces involved.

The educator often overvalues the significance of psychology for remedial training. For well-rounded work, he must take into consideration many other factors, psychiatric, sociological, economic, and cultural.

TWO

THE ANALYSIS OF A
SYMPTOM

THE general survey in our first chapter has given us
some idea of the task of child guidance and has introduced
us to psychoanalysis. At this point, we could continue the
theoretical discussion of our work, leaving the application
until a later period. Our discussion would then divide itself
into two parts: the first would establish general principles
and serve as a foundation, the second would show the application of these principles to specific cases. This procedure
would have several advantages; in the first place, a sys-
tematic introduction would familiarize us with the psychoanalytic way of thinking so that we would not find our
conclusions shocking or far-fetched as is often the case in
the first approach. In the second place, the presentation of
cases would be facilitated, since in showing the relation
between cause and treatment of dissocial behaviour we could
refer to the theory already learned instead of having to
interrupt our story for explanations. This method seems
a logical approach to the subject. Despite these advantages,
I wish to suggest another method. I am in the midst of
practical work with children, and theoretical discussions
without application seem to me out of place. Because I
see greater advantages in bringing you face to face with

11

real situations, I prefer to risk the dangers already mentioned: that you will be incredulous, that the interpolations of theory will interrupt the story, and that you may criticize me for being unscientific. I shall present problems as I have found them, neither made to order nor simplified. We shall learn what each case demands in the way of special knowledge, psychoanalytic or otherwise.

Let us begin with a simple case in the clinic rather than in the institution. A mother brought her thirteen-year-old son to the clinic, complaining about his misbehaviour and insisting that he be sent to a reformatory. I first interviewed the mother, who told a well-rounded story with the help of a few direct questions. On Wednesday, the boy had taken some soap, soda, and the newspaper into the laundry of the apartment house where the family lived. When she returned to the apartment at noon, she found the door locked. The boy had disappeared, leaving the key with a neighbour. The mother said, "I thought he had run away because he has done so several times before without any reason. We are good to him at home. . . . There was nothing missing from my purse which was on the table. There was quite a little money in it. My husband's savings had not been touched either. They are kept in the inside pocket of an old coat that hangs in the closet. The boy knew this. I did not discover until later that he had taken some money out of the drawer of the kitchen table and all there was in his sister's savings bank. When he did not come home that night, I went to the police and reported him as missing. On Friday afternoon, when I was coming home with some work, I met him near the house. He was stubborn and sulky but he had washed and had on clean clothes. He wouldn't talk and I couldn't get out of him where he had been or what he had done with the money. I don't know yet. I didn't scold him or whip him, but I can't do anything more with him. He belongs in a reform school."

She discussed the home conditions quite frankly. She had been happily married for fifteen years to a foreman in a machine shop. She did home embroidery for a firm in the city. When I asked if there were ever marital disputes, she said, "Oh yes, little scraps such as everyone has." The relationship between her and the boy seemed to be good. "I am sure he loves me more than he loves his father. My husband is much too easy on him. He lets the boy do almost anything he wants and practically never punishes him. I get awfully annoyed about this, but it does no good. If I say anything, my husband leaves the house and does not come back for hours. We can't give much time to the children because both of us work all day. My husband loves to fish and usually goes fishing on Sunday. He often takes the boy along. My daughter and I stay at home and do the mending and darning."

The family lived in three rooms. The daughter slept with the parents; the boy in a tiny bedroom. The mother had had no trouble with the daughter, who was eleven, got along well in school, and was industrious at home. When the two children quarrelled, the girl gave in to her brother more than she should. The woman concluded her story by saying that there had been no quarrel of any kind before the boy ran away this time; he had no reason to be afraid of punishment, and she knew of nothing else that could have frightened him. She could not explain his running away. It was out of the question that he had been enticed by other boys; his only friend was a boy of a nice family, and he was hardly ever on the streets.

The following facts supplemented the woman's story. Both parents were in good health; there was no alcoholism or insanity on either side of the family, nor any indication of criminal or delinquent tendencies. The boy's development had been normal; he did not have convulsions as a child and there was nothing now to make one suspect any psychic illness.

I then interviewed the boy. I asked the mother to wait, assuring her that I would tell her later what seemed best to do. The boy made a good first impression. There was no trace of the typical delinquent in his appearance; on the contrary, he looked like a well-brought-up child of good middle-class family. Although overgrown, he seemed strong, and there was a sunny smile on his round, childish face. His dark hair was neatly parted; his face and hands looked as if they had been scrubbed. His immaculate white sailor suit enhanced the impression of an overgrown child.

After the usual greeting and a few opening remarks, we sat down at a table in my office. When we discuss the relationship between mentor and child in a later chapter, we shall take up the importance of the first interview. A part of our conversation I shall repeat verbatim; the remainder can be summarized. All interviews in the clinic are private. The boy cast a different light on the relationship between his parents; there was not much harmony between them; they did not understand each other very well. When the mother was angry, his father would go away and stay for hours at a time. A week ago Saturday after a quarrel, his father took his fishing tackle and went to the country. Instead of returning at the usual time, he stayed away until late Sunday night. His mother feared something had happened to him and was much worried.

The boy's attitude toward his parents was ambivalent; it wavered between affection and rejection. When his mother was too strict, he turned to his father; if his father refused to take him fishing, he complained to his mother. He loved his mother more, but he thought his father was right to go away when there were unpleasant quarrels at home. His sister was not very nice to him; he often got angry with her. His mother seemed to favour his sister; on the Tuesday evening before he ran away, his mother had given his sister money to have her shoes resoled; she did not give him anything although he needed new shoes more than his sister. And his mother did not see why he should be annoyed about this. His sister got better grades in school than he. He did not like school; he would much rather quit and learn to be a mechanic. He had few friends other than one boy of his own age whom he liked very much. Except when this friend called for him to go walking with him, he did not enjoy going out on the street. Sometimes they went to movies together. He liked travel pictures best and he enjoyed travel books. The only reason he wished to become a mechanic was that his parents would not let him go to sea.

I shall repeat our conversation about his running away, in so far as it clarifies the picture of his delinquency.

"When did you run away?"

"On Wednesday."

"When was it exactly, in the morning or in the afternoon?"

"I'm not sure how late it was, but toward noon, before lunch."

"Did you start from home or were you out on the street?"

"I was at home and left from there."

"Was anyone else at home?"

"No, I was alone."

"Where were the others?"

"Mother was in the laundry, father was at the factory, and my sister was at school."

"Do you remember if anything was wrong beforehand, were you frightened or angry?"

"No."

"Perhaps something happened Tuesday evening."

"No."

"What did you do Tuesday evening?"

"I went to the store. Mother had given me some money. I brought back some change and she put it in the table drawer."

"Now think a minute, wasn't your father or your mother angry with you on Tuesday evening or Wednesday morning?"

"No."

"Did you have any trouble with your father?"

"No."

"Or with your sister?"

"No; oh yes, I was mad at her because she could have her shoes resoled before I got new ones."

"How was that?"

"Mother gave her some money and she put it in her savings bank."

"Why?"

"I don't know. Mother took the money out of the table drawer."

"Did you think about running away on Tuesday night?"

"No."

"When was it then?"

"Not until Wednesday and then I left right away."

"What did you do beforehand?"

"I took some soda and soap and the newspaper to mother in the laundry. Then I went back to the apartment."

"Did you look at the paper?"

"Yes."

"What did you read about?"

"That a man was lost in the mountains."

"When you took the things to your mother, was anything wrong?"

"Mother was cross on account of the stamps."

"What stamps?"

"My friend had had some stamps stolen and they thought that I had taken them."

"Who are 'they'?"

"Oh, everyone, but mother, too."

"Were you mad at your mother?"

"Of course. I thought to myself, 'She makes me tired.' "

"When you went home from the laundry, what did you do?"

"I spread a piece of bread with margarine and ate it."

"Were you in the kitchen or in the living room then?"

"I was looking out of the window in the living room."

"Did you notice anything on the street?"

"I was looking into the court. There was a dog down there and I threw him a piece of bread."

"Show me how you stood by the window."

The boy then leaned over the table on his elbows. I let him remain in this position to make it easier for him to remember.

"What happened after you had thrown the bread to the dog?"

"Then I ran away."

"Wait a minute, not so fast. You were leaning on the window sill, had finished your bread and margarine, had thrown some to the dog. Now think a bit and try to remember why all of a sudden you wanted to run away."

"I don't know."

"Did the idea come to you while you were eating?"

"After I had finished, I thought, 'I'll go to Tulln.' "

"Why to Tulln?"

"Because I wanted to go to the woods."

"Are there woods only in Tulln?"

"No, but I wanted to get some cherries for my mother."

"But why just in Tulln?"

"Because father owns some cherry trees there."

"How do you know that?"

"Because I was with him when he bought them. I have often been in Tulln with my father when he went fishing."

"I see. You thought you would go to Tulln to get cherries for your mother, and what then?"

"There were some cherry stones lying on the window sill. Then I went into the kitchen and made myself four bread-and-margarine sandwiches."

"What else did you do?"

"I took some of mother's money and a bag."

"Where did you get the money?"

"Out of the kitchen table drawer."

"Are you sure?"

"Yes."

"Now think a minute."

"I took all there was in the drawer."

"Where did you get the rest?"

"Out of my sister's savings bank."

"Where was the bank?"

"In the chest in the living room."

"Was it locked?"

"Yes, but the key was in mother's purse."

"Where was the purse?"

"On the table in the living room."

"Was there money in it?"

"Yes."

"How much?"

"I don't know."

"Did you take all the money in your sister's bank, or did you leave some?"

"I did not take it all."

"Why not?"

"I didn't need any more for the trip."

"Was there money in any other place in the apartment?"

"Yes, in the closet in an old coat of father's. He keeps his money in an old billfold in the pocket."

"Was this closet locked?"

"Yes, but the key was in the lock."

"Have you a bank, too?"

"Yes."

"Why didn't you take your money?"

"Because I wanted to save it."

"How did you happen to take your sister's money?"

No answer.

"Don't you want to tell me?"

No answer.

"You took the money out of your sister's bank, and what then?"

"I put the sandwiches in my pocket and locked the apartment."

"Did you take the key along?"

"No, I gave it to a neighbour, and then I left."

"Weren't you afraid you would meet your mother on the stairs?"

"No, she had said she would have to hurry in order to finish by lunch time."

"What would she have done?"

"I don't know. I was supposed to put the lunch on to warm."

"Did you do that?"

"No."

"Where did you go when you left home?"

"To the station."

"Did you walk or take the street car?"

"I walked, and then I had to wait for two hours."

"What did you do in the station?"

"I sat down and ate a sandwich."

"Did your father always carry some lunch when you and he went fishing together?"

"Yes; and I always had to carry it."

"When you were at the station, were you afraid that you might be caught?"

"No, nobody from home ever goes there."

"Did you know when you reached Tulln?"

"Yes, I know the Tulln station very well."

"What did you do when you got to Tulln?"

"Nothing."

"Did you stay in the station?"

"No, I went right to the woods."

"But then you did do something."

"Yes, I thought you meant, did I get into any mischief."

"What did you do in the woods?"

"I found the cherry trees."

"Did you pick any cherries?"

"No, they weren't ripe yet, and then I was afraid to go home."

"What did you do then?"

"I walked around in the woods."

"Why?"

"Because I was hunting strawberries. There were other cherry trees there, too. I took some cherries and ate them."

"Did you take some from these trees for your mother?"

"No."

"How long did you stay in the woods?"

"Until it was quite dark. It began to rain, too."

"Where did you go that night?"

"I slept in a barn."

He now described more in detail how he spent the night, and how careful he had to be in order to avoid being discovered by the farmer. He told how lonely he was because he had to sleep all by himself in the hay; said at first he was frightened lest he not wake up in time in the morning and be caught by the farmer; then he could not sleep at all and so he left the barn as soon as it was light. Although it continued to rain all day, he remained in the woods so as not to be detected. He did not think much about home. His only concern was whether he could sleep in the same barn that night. He waited until it was dark, crept back to the barn and crawled up into the hay without being seen. This time he slept very well and did not wake up until it was broad daylight. He had to wait until the farmer left the house and then he ran back to the woods in a hurry. He had not spent any of the remaining money but saved it for the return trip; strawberries, cherries, and his three sandwiches had been his only food. He ate the last sandwich on Friday morning when it was already quite hard. It was hunger that drove him home. On the trip home, he felt no particular remorse. He did not feel afraid until he reached the door. His sister, who was the only one at home, said that his mother would soon be back from work, and that his parents were very angry about his running away. He washed, put on clean clothes, and went to meet his mother. When he met her on the street, she did not scold him but simply said he was such a bad boy that he would have to be put in a reform school.

Another short talk with the mother confirmed the boy's story. After hearing the reasons which the boy gave, she was inclined to view the stealing and the running away as not at all serious. But she could not understand why he had not told her this himself. To answer this question, we must examine the affair more closely. Is the matter so simple as the mother thought? Even a superficial consideration enables us to recognize two distinct phases in his behaviour, the product of different psychic situations. The boy himself told us where the one ended and the other began: in the woods when he saw that the cherries were not ripe. "The cherries weren't ripe and then I was afraid to go home." Let us leave the second phase for the time being and return to the beginning. We can eliminate several possible causes of the delinquency at once. There is no indication of illness nor any inherent tendencies toward vagrancy. Neither is it possible to explain the running away as a result of fear of punishment, or as an anxiety reaction. One thing is certain: the boy explained his action by his wish to get cherries for his mother.

Let us first discuss the case without any psychoanalytic consideration. No child is absolutely trustworthy, so we must weigh the boy's statements carefully. We do not yet know whether he told the truth. The statements of delinquents should always be checked. However, when we catch a child in a lie, we should not shame him. Expressions such as "You lie," "You must tell the truth," should always be avoided. It is much more efficacious to act as if the child had made a mistake. We can say, for example, "Are you sure you meant what you said?" "Now think a minute," or "Take your time; tell me again," etc.

How was it in this boy's case? Did he really wish to bring cherries to his mother from Tulln, or did he tell me this only as an excuse, or what was his motive? Since we cannot determine this with certainty, we must be satisfied with establishing its probability on the basis of our general impression of the boy. Did he lie? It is possible. He had refused to give his mother any explanation and he knew she had brought him to me to be sent to a reformatory. His fate therefore depended on the impression he made on me. He might have thought, "If I am clever, I can get out of this trouble." If he was guided by this idea, then he understood his mother very well. Her attitude had changed after she learned from me that a loving thought had prompted the boy's running away. Does the rest of his conduct make us feel that this was the case? Yes, because he said first that he wanted to go to Tulln to get to the woods and only later mentioned the cherry trees. Do you recall this part of the interview? After I had made several attempts to find out when he had decided to go to Tulln, our conversation was as follows: "Did the idea [to go to Tulln] come to you while you were eating?" "After I had finished, I thought, 'I'll go to Tulln.' " "Why to Tulln?" "*Because I wanted to go to the woods.*" Not until I asked, "Are there woods only in Tulln?" did it occur to him . . . "No, but I wanted to get some cherries for my mother." "But why just in Tulln?" "*Because Father owns some cherry trees there.*"

Let us now consider without prejudice whether he might have told the truth. This seems probable when we compare his statements with those of his mother, who was certainly not in collusion with him. The two are in complete agreement about all the facts. The boy's telling me that he stole some cherries from trees which did not belong to his father reveals a streak of honesty. He told this spontaneously although he could have thought that this would work to his disadvantage. To this can be added the facts that he took with him a bag for the cherries, that he appropriated no more of the easily accessible money than he needed for the railway fare, that he spent nothing on himself but saved the remainder for the return trip, and that he was seized by fright when he discovered that he could not carry out his plan because the cherries were not ripe. When we consider the impression that he made in the interview, it seems impossible to believe that he was lying. And yet the assumption that he was telling the truth is equally unsatisfactory. There seems to be no reason why he should have thought affectionately of his mother. On the contrary, he had been annoyed with her the evening before because his sister was to get shoes before he did, and just before running away, he had been angry about the stamps.

But perhaps he was a "good child." After his anger had cooled off and his hunger was satisfied, he thought about his poor mother working in the laundry and he felt sorry for her. Getting the cherries was an act of conciliation. This assumption would seem admissible were it not refuted by another fact: he stole from his mother and sister. If bringing cherries to his mother had been his only idea, he could have done this more simply by buying some with his savings. Nor would it have been necessary to come home empty-handed; just as he stole cherries for himself, so he might have filled the bag with stolen cherries for his mother. Did he lie after all? We are not yet obliged to believe this. Perhaps his sweet tooth was the cause even though he was unaware of it. By that I mean: he had eaten his bread, he wanted something more, he saw some cherry stones on the window sill and conceived the idea of getting some cherries for his mother. His own desire for cherries disguised itself in this form. His theft would be socially acceptable because he spent none of the money for himself. He would naturally get some of the cherries. But had his appetite been strong enough to make him steal, it would hardly have suffered the delayed satisfaction occasioned by the long wait in the station and the ride to Tulln. He would have yielded to it earlier and bought something to eat. It would have been easy for him to take more money to satisfy his desires. He subsisted on berries and his three sandwiches for three days, he spent no money on food, and he did not steal money elsewhere. We know cases in which stealing is the result of uninhibited appetite, but this does not seem to be one of them. We can hardly say that the boy lied, but we cannot maintain that he told the truth. We are tempted to compromise, to say that although he told untruths, he believed them to be the truth. Is this possible and can we proceed on such an uncertain assumption? The uncertainty increases when I raise the question which I have so far purposely overlooked: why the boy spent the money taken from his sister's bank and none of his own nor of his mother's or father's although it was equally accessible.

We seem to have reached an impasse. Perhaps you are thinking of other ways of explaining the boy's conduct; perhaps you are impatiently asking why all this fuss simply because a boy stole some money and ran away from home. We have set ourselves the task of investigating this dissocial behaviour; we cannot abandon it just because we are not satisfied with the results. It seems we must turn to psychoanalysis for help. From the psychoanalytic point of view, it becomes impossible to consider the stealing and the running away as accidental, nor can the boy's affection for his mother or his sweet tooth be accepted as the cause. Where shall we find the motive?

Up until now, we have concerned ourselves with only one

of the boy's statements. Since this leads nowhere, let us consider another. When he took the soda and soap to his mother in the laundry, she made a remark about the stamps which his friend had lost. He was very angry at being suspected and thought to himself, "She makes me tired," which could be interpreted to mean, "She doesn't like me; I am going to get out of here." Where would this wish originate? He had been annoyed with his mother the evening before because of the shoes and now she had vexed him again. He had to do something to change the uncomfortable situation in which he found himself. An impulse to run away is understandable. But this does not explain the stealing, nor why he took money just from his sister and mother, nor why he chose to go to Tulln and said that he had planned to get cherries for his mother. We must go a step farther and be willing to admit that he might have been unconscious of his real purpose. If he does not know what determined his action, then these reasons are not in his consciousness. We cannot elucidate them by questioning him, not because he does not wish to tell us but because he himself does not know them. They must be sought in the boy's unconscious.

We have already spoken of the dynamic concept in psychoanalysis, that is, that psychic phenomena are the product of psychic forces. The boy's trip to Tulln and all that went with it can be regarded as the result of such a process. We must therefore discover the psychic drive behind this behaviour. It would seem that there were two drives at work, both in the unconscious, and that one is operating to prevent the other from becoming conscious. The final solution of the boy's dissocial act depends on the uncovering of this contest between psychic forces. But we should know more about the psychic processes concerned. We shall therefore leave the discussion of the specific problem for the moment and turn to a more general study of psychic phenomena.

We should begin with a brief discussion of the unconscious. We must not think of the unconscious simply as an aid in explaining psychic phenomena, but rather as actually existent, just as consciousness is. We then understand that it has its special significance and special functions. When we think of the conscious and the unconscious, we do not mean two definitely separated compartments of the mind, which can be so designated. However, psychic processes, as such, do separate themselves into two phases, which are differentiated according to whether one "knows" or is "conscious" of them or not. The unconscious, in which all kinds of things are harboured, has various functions to perform. For example, our wishes come from this source, and our emotional attitudes toward people and things around us. What we call attraction to another person is present in the unconscious long before we are aware of it. If we observe the reaction of the new-born child to his organic needs and to the stimuli which come from outside himself, we understand why Freud recognized the unconscious processes as primary. There is little of consciousness to be seen in the infant. As the child grows, he becomes aware of his bodily sensations, conveyed to him through his sense organs; thus consciousness evolves out of the unconscious.

The tendency of the child to imitate is also a function of the unconscious. Feelings of love for his parents develop in the child without his knowledge. On account of this, he admires and assumes certain of their characteristics. We say he identifies himself with them. Imitation is doing what others do in identification with them. When a little girl treats her doll as she has seen her mother treat a younger brother or sister, or plays at housekeeping with her toy dishes, she is identifying herself with her mother. The little boy who puts on his father's hat and parades through the room with his father's walking stick, or refuses to go to bed because his father has not yet retired, is identifying himself with his father. If we observe children closely, we find ourselves continually confronted with these identifications. Children identify themselves not only with persons but also with animals and occasionally with inanimate objects, such as toys.

Why are we now concerned with this tendency in the child? Because this characteristic, although it does not explain our boy's behaviour, gives us a hint as to the way he solved the conflict with his mother. We know that his father left home after quarrels with his wife and that he stayed away for some time. By identifying himself with his father and doing as he did, he escaped his own unpleasant situation. He went to Tulln. He was simply repeating what his father had done the previous Sunday. In addition, he took revenge on his mother by causing her distress. He must have thought that his mother would worry about his disappearance just as someone must have worried about the man who was lost in the mountains. His revenge was made greater by stealing money from his mother and sister. In this way, he settled the score with his sister for the favouritism shown her on the day before; if the money was gone, she could not get shoes before he did.

Maybe you agree with these conclusions on the basis of a father identification, but perhaps you do not understand why he did not admit this; why, instead of saying that he had been angry with his mother, he told me that he wanted to be kind to her, to bring her a present of cherries. You are justified in feeling that identification does not explain the stealing and furthermore that all this sounds like quite a complicated thought process for a simple boy. But we must advance step by step in explaining his motives.

It will be easier if we do not insist on discovering a single motive behind the boy's actions but rather admit the possibility that several impulses united to determine them. Let us imagine that a wish demanding gratification rises in the unconscious. The following is an example. A child stands beside a table on which there is a box of candy. If he has never been told that it is wrong to take candy without asking permission, he will help himself to a piece and enjoy it without conflict. In this case, the wish meets no opposition. Another child has been forbidden to eat candy, but he has forgotten this. A vague feeling of uneasiness will make him hesitate, but he finally takes the candy and eats it without a bad conscience. In this case, the wish meets with weak opposition. A third child understands clearly that he should not take the candy, but he wants it so much that he takes it anyhow and then suffers guilty feelings. In this case, the wish overcame the restraint. Another possible reaction is that an inhibiting force, the result of the child's training, will immediately drive the wish back into the unconscious or even prevent it from ever becoming conscious. In general, we can say that whenever a wish conflicts with a moral, religious, or social principle, the latter exerts pressure either to make the wish remain unconscious or to repress it into the unconscious after it has been conscious. Two forces play a part in the mechanism of repression: the unconscious, which aims toward gratification, and the conscious, which tries to prevent the gratification; in other words, a repressed and a repressing force. The result of this conflict is not predictable. The repressed impulse may be strong enough to overthrow the opposition of the repressing impulse, or the reverse may be the case. Let us imagine that neither is strong enough completely to conquer the other. This situation must manifest itself in some way. A banal example will illustrate. In our professional work, we are often subjected to annoyances. It would be a relief if we could rid ourselves of the accumulated affect by scolding someone, but our training in good manners restrains us. Two tendencies are now at odds in us. If the first conquers, we indulge in an outburst of temper; if the second proves stronger, we keep silent. But maybe neither of these two things happens. Instead we are seized by a violent fit of coughing. What does this mean? It represents a compromise between the two impulses. Scolding is a motor mechanism for affect discharge through the muscles of speech. Coughing employs the same muscles but in a way which escapes the disapproval of our better selves. Such an expression, which unites two tendencies, psychoanalysis calls a symptom. We see that both tendencies contribute to the formation of the symptom, or, as Freud expresses it, the symptom is supported from both sides, from the repressed and from the repressing. Such symptom formations often appear as manifestations of neurotic illness. Similarly certain acts of the healthy individual are attributable to this mechanism. Freud has made a study of some of these everyday phenomena which are known in psychoanalysis as blunders, slips of speech, and the like.

The foregoing example of symptom formation as a compromise between conflicting forces brings us back to our patient. May we attribute his behaviour to the same mechanism? Do we find here two opposing tendencies which find expression in a symptom because neither is strong enough to overthrow the other? If this is the case, we should be able to determine the repressed and the repressing forces and the symptom which they created. There is certainly no doubt that the boy was at odds with his mother before he ran away. Let us now assume that his desire to run away, to do what his father had done, contained the one impulse. This impulse might have remained conscious or it might have been repressed into the unconscious by some inhibiting force within the boy which opposed the running away. In the first instance, he would have gone to Tulln and he would have known why he went. A powerful opposing impulse might have repressed this wish and have resulted in his

staying at home. Its content might have been, "A decent
boy does not run away" or "I'll get a whipping for running
away." But the fact is that he ran away.

Let us try another approach for the purpose of discovering conflicting impulses. We found that the boy's anger
with his mother culminated in the revengeful wish to punish
her. This impulse could hardly remain conscious; it probably would not have been permitted to become conscious before being repressed; the command to love one's mother is
strongly entrenched in every child. If these two impulses
actually existed in the boy, what would have happened?
Had revenge conquered scruple, he would have stolen and
run away, but he would have known the reason. Had moral
training triumphed, there would have been no delinquency,
as we have already indicated. If neither conquered, we
should have had a situation favourable for producing
a symptom. A symptom could be formed out of a revengeful and a moral impulse provided that both could find
partial satisfaction in a single act. The boy's journey to
Tulln represents such a solution. We can imagine that the
conflict which took place while he stood by the window eating his bread and margarine came to an end when he saw
the cherry stones on the window sill and resolved to go to
Tulln. We know he wanted revenge. His identification
with his father makes it possible for him to imitate him and
to choose his father's method of causing his mother worry
and distress. The moral impulse, to do something nice for
his mother, is not capable of thwarting the gratification of

the revenge, but it serves to change the conscious form of
the revenge by adding a motive of kindness. The idea of
bringing cherries is united with the other purpose; the
symptom is complete. His delinquent act is not possible
until it has been disguised in this way. This symptom differs
from the usual neurotic symptom in that it does not have
the quality of discomfort and unpleasantness which characterize the neurotic symptom. It is this pain which makes
the neurotic aware of his illness and ready for treatment.
The fact that the delinquent does not suffer discomfort
from his symptoms constitutes one of the chief difficulties
in the analytic treatment of delinquents.

At the expense of considerable effort, we have discovered
that a delinquent act is founded on the same mechanism
which we regularly find in the neurotic symptom. Although
we must not make the mistake of thinking that every delinquency can be explained in the same way, nevertheless we
can consider that we have already learned a great deal
about diagnosis. This discussion has also contributed to our
knowledge of therapeutic treatment. We now know that we
cannot content ourselves with the first superficial statements about a case such as "A boy has stolen and run away."
We must learn the exact circumstances. Nor is it sufficient
for discovering the causes of the delinquency to question
the boy, the parents, and others in the environment, since
they do not know the real significance of the dissocial behaviour. Without psychoanalytic training the worker cannot unearth these hidden factors. In the case of our boy,

nothing could have been accomplished with kind words or with punishment; either course would have aggravated his hate impulses. This dissocial behaviour was of a compulsive nature and not to be changed except by altering the forces which determined it.

THREE
SOME CAUSES OF DELINQUENCY

THE conclusions reached in the analysis of a symptom in the previous chapter do not justify us in attributing all dissocial behaviour to the same mechanism. I emphasize this because the prevalent tendency toward generalization is especially dangerous for the social worker. The satisfaction derived from having used a therapeutic measure successfully may mislead him into drawing analogous conclusions about the next patient who behaves in the same way. He may work with a child for weeks without success and then find that he has not made his diagnosis on the basis of the child's reactions but has unconsciously adapted them to a preconception of the case and has overlooked everything that did not fit into his theoretical construction.

It is not superfluous to remind you that you should meet each case without preconceptions and should not seek in every delinquent an opportunity for making psychoanalytic discoveries. Every dissocial child is not the "interesting problem" you are looking for. You should always try the simplest measures first. If you observe carefully the effect of your therapy step by step, you are sure to find in the course of the treatment the deeper problems which must be solved. You should not be disturbed if everything is not cleared up; even the worker thoroughly trained in psychoanalysis still finds many things he cannot explain.

In this brief discussion, it seems more important to present cases which will show the diverse character of dissocial behaviour rather than to make an exhaustive study of any one type.

First, let us ask the question: can we make any general formula out of what we have learned up to this point? If we regard all behaviour as the result of psychic forces in the psychoanalytic sense, then we must think of dissocial behaviour, too, as so determined, and we can express the desired formula thus: dissocial behaviour indicates that the psychic processes which determine behaviour are not functioning harmoniously. This formulation enables us to define the problem of delinquency psychoanalytically and points the way toward a solution. Delinquency can now be considered as a dynamic expression; it can be attributed to the interplay of psychic forces, which have created the distortion which we call dissocial behaviour. For example, the stealing and running away of the boy in the previous chapter were the result of psychic forces which found no socially acceptable outlet and therefore forced him to behaviour which was at odds with society. We then term him dissocial.

When we look at dissocial behaviour, or symptoms of delinquency, as distinct from delinquency, we see the same relation as that between the symptoms of a disease and the disease itself. This parallel enables us to regard truancy, vagrancy, stealing, and the like as symptoms of delinquency, just as fever, inflammation, and pain are symptoms of disease. If the physician limits himself to clearing up symptoms, he does not necessarily cure the disease. The possibility of a new illness may remain; new symptoms may replace the old. In the re-education of the delinquent, we have an analogous situation. Our task is to remove the cause rather than to eliminate the overt behaviour. Although this seems obvious, it is little understood. Our experience in the guidance clinic and in the training school is that the *symptoms* of delinquency and the fundamental problem underlying delinquency are constantly confused. What parents undertake by way of correction or punishment serves only to suppress the dissocial behaviour. If this behaviour disappears, the problem is considered solved. However, the disappearance of a symptom does not indicate a cure. When a psychic process is denied expression and the psychic energies determining it remain undischarged, a new path of discharge will be found along the line of least resistance, and a new form of delinquency will result. It is even possible that a nervous symptom will develop. More often, however, it appears as if the psychic energies had gathered new force. Following a period of socially acceptable behaviour, the original signs of delinquency often reappear, more deeply anchored and more pronounced. The cases which come to the clinic usually show this recurrence of symptoms.

This conception of behaviour as dynamically determined enables us to correct another common mistake. When I ask parents how they account for the dissocial behaviour of their children, I usually receive the answer that it is a result of bad company and running around on the streets.

To a certain extent this is true, but thousands of other children grow up under the same unfavourable circumstances and still are not delinquent. There must be something in the child himself which the environment brings out in the form of delinquency. If for the moment we call this unknown something a predisposition to delinquency, we have the factor without which an unfavourable environment can have no power over the child.

We like to think that this predisposition is inherited. Psychoanalysis has shown us that heredity cannot explain everything, that the first experiences of childhood are important in determining later development. The predisposition to delinquency is not a finished product at birth but is determined by the emotional relationships, that is, by the first experiences which the environment forces upon the child. This does not mean that every child so predisposed will become delinquent. Bad company, street influences, and the like, factors which are not the underlying causes of delinquency but the direct or indirect provocation, also play a part.

Through his conduct, the delinquent exposes himself continually to the danger of punishment. Why he persists in this behaviour does not yet interest us; we are concerned now with the fact that his behaviour is contrary to the demands of reality. This does not surprise the psychoanalyst. He knows that the neurotic has a reality of his own. Why should the delinquent not have a special brand of reality, too? This brings new light on the subject of delinquency, renders it accessible to the psychoanalytic

method of investigation, and allows us to employ psychoanalytic terms. We can now speak of the overt bad behaviour as "manifest" delinquency. When the same state
exists but has not yet expressed itself, we speak of "latent"
delinquency.

Delinquency is manifest when it develops into dissocial
behaviour. The boy who plays truant, runs away, or steals
is manifestly delinquent; the boy in whom these expressions
lie dormant is in the stage of latent delinquency. Suitable
circumstances only are needed to turn latent into manifest
delinquency. We see now the bearing bad company has on
the real problem. To find the causes of delinquency we must
not only seek the provocation which made the latent delinquency manifest but we must also determine what created the latent delinquency. It is the task of re-education
to weaken the latent tendency to delinquency. Later we
shall learn that this is tantamount to altering the ego structure of the child. When we realize that the provocation to
delinquency is confused with its cause, that symptoms are
mistaken for the disease, we understand why there are so
many false conceptions of what should be done with the
delinquent child and we wonder no longer that treatment
often fails. Without the discovery of the deep underlying
causes of delinquency, any cure is accidental.

The following cases come with one exception from the
institution.[1] The first is a sixteen-year-old boy. The case
history related that he had gone to live with a married
sister after the death of his mother, that the sister had

---

[1] The correctional institution at Ober Hollabrunn.

neglected him, that he had lived on the streets and become delinquent. The chief complaints were vagrancy and refusal to work. The decision of the psychiatric clinic was: "Should be sent to the training school." The fact that the report contained no statement of special significance seemed to indicate that mental disease was out of the question. The boy's final school report, from the sixth grade, showed a grade of 1 in deportment, 2 in industry, and 2 in progress. He was behind his normal class because he had entered school late. His record indicated that he was at least of normal intelligence. Since his deportment was graded 1, we judged that his vagrancy had begun after school was out; otherwise he would have been marked down for truancy. In an intelligence test, he was found to be normal. However, in the Aschaffenburg Test, he did poorly. This test is as follows: the child must close his eyes and for a period of three minutes say the words that come to mind. The result is set down after every half minute. The average number of words in the prescribed time is sixty-five. This boy was far under average; he gave only sixteen words and these with hesitation. This unusually inhibited flow of ideas corresponded to the general impression which he made. He was well developed physically, he was not unattractive in appearance, but his movements were sluggish. He was polite, but shy and reserved. His uncommunicativeness indicated a very passive nature. To all appearances, he was a gentle boy, a harmless delinquent who would be easy to manage.

The following are a few of the most significant statements that he made during interviews over a period of months. "My father was a labourer, and he died in a hospital." He remembered the exact date of his father's death the first time we spoke of it. "I was awfully sorry for my mother because she was left alone." "I have a sister about fifteen years older than I am; four brothers and sisters died. I never knew them." "We lived in two rooms. I slept between mother and father in their bed. My sister slept on the sofa." "When she got married, I was twelve years old, but I kept on sleeping with my parents." "When my father died, I took his place in bed and I began to take care of my mother." "I always cleaned up the house, made the fires, and started the dinner before my mother came from the factory." "In 19—— my mother died."

The first statements about his mother's death were made calmly, as if it were something that did not affect him. He said nothing whatever concerning the manner of her death. The details came later with some tears, but even then without any strong emotion. The date of her death he recalled comparatively late. She had suffered a horrible death; she had been caught in a machine and her body had been badly mangled. The boy had received the news without any warning. "It was about noon. I was at home and a woman came and said that my mother had fainted in the factory." "I went to the factory right away with my sister and they told us at the office what had happened to my mother. It made me so sick that I fell over. When I came to, my sister was standing beside me. She said she had already been to the morgue and then we went home together." "She sat up with

me all night because I was so scared, and she wouldn't let
me go to the funeral. I played with my Matador set because
I couldn't cry and mother had always liked it when I made
something nice." "Then I moved to my sister's house; our
furniture was sold, and my sister and I divided the money.
She wouldn't let me pay her anything for board, but I'll
pay her back when I begin to earn." "I was apprenticed to
a mechanic in July and was there for two months. I couldn't
enjoy anything. I couldn't help thinking all the time about
my mother and how awful she must have looked after the
accident, and then I ran away from my work." "Then I
went to work for an innkeeper in the country. We did our
own butchering there and I felt so sorry for the animals I
couldn't bear it and so I ran away again." "Then I was with
a carpenter but I didn't like that, either. My guardian was
mad at me and said I was lazy and would have to go to a
reform school." "I found another place myself but I didn't
stay long. I don't know why. I just couldn't stand it."
"Most of the time I spent in the park watching the soldiers
drill. Lots of people were there and I liked that. The nicest
thing was when the band played, marching at the head of
the company. I always followed them." "My guardian and
my sister kept telling me I must learn something, so I
wouldn't go home at night but stayed away and slept under
the bridge. Often I was arrested and taken to the police station." "My guardian said he couldn't stand it any longer
seeing me go to the bad and one day he took me to the
Juvenile Court, but they didn't keep me there and we went
home again. A week later, a man came to the house and took

me to the railway station where there were a lot of boys and girls and we all went away on the train together."

During his stay in the training school, this boy made no particular friends among the pupils or the teachers. Neither did he develop a close relationship to me, although he became more communicative during our frequent talks together. His singular attitude toward his comrades showed up most clearly whenever a pupil got into mischief. He seemed always to be able to get the matter settled in such a way that no one's feelings were hurt, the teachers did not scold, and the guilty boy got off without punishment. In spite of the fact that his intelligence was higher than that of the boys with whom he worked, he did not try to become a leader. He was proud of his knowledge of farming, the work to which he was assigned. He considered his greatest fault to be forgetfulness. During his stay, his depression disappeared almost completely. He became less forgetful; he worked more diligently, although he continued to be very slow; and he showed no need to make friends. He stayed with us until the institution was dissolved; then he found a place on a large farm and from that time on showed no further signs of delinquency.

A few words concerning the psychology of neurosis are in order at this point. Some people are unable to assimilate a shocking experience of great emotional content. Unprepared for a sudden, overpowering shock, they cannot react to it in a normal way. Such an experience can act as a blow and can so injure the psychic mechanisms that they are permanently damaged. When a highly emotional experience has such a consequence, we say that it has operated traumatically. We refer to it also as a psychic trauma. Under certain conditions, such an experience will produce a neurosis. From Freud [2] we have learned, "The traumatic neuroses demonstrate very clearly that a fixation to the moment of the traumatic occurrence lies at their root. . . . It is as though these persons had not yet been able to deal adequately with the situation, as if this task were still actually before them unaccomplished."

The case we are now considering shows vagrancy and refusal to work as indications of delinquency. These are given as reasons for his being committed to the institution. The symptoms appeared after the death of his mother, shortly after he went to live with his sister, and they grew visibly worse until his commitment. According to our formulation, the latent delinquency must have existed before he went to his sister's; in other words, before there was any overt dissocial behaviour. We must seek the causes of the latent tendencies in the boy's constitution and in his childhood and other experiences, just as we do in the case of the neurotic. We know nothing that indicates a constitutional abnormality. Since the boy was not analysed, we are not acquainted with his earlier experiences. But some things we do know. The boy was told without warning of the hideous death of his mother. He was so shocked by this that he fainted. The sister had to sit up with him all night because

---

[2] *Introductory Lectures on Psycho-Analysis,* translated by Joan Riviere, revised edition, 1929, p. 232. London: George Allen and Unwin, Ltd.

of his fright. The fact that he was not permitted to go to the funeral indicates that those about him recognized the severity of his condition. This condition is again reflected in his playing with his Matador set while his mother was being buried, certainly not normal behaviour for a fourteen-year-old boy. In the office of the factory, this boy had suffered a trauma that resulted in a permanent psychic injury. He confirmed the fact that this trauma bears relation to his running away from work. "I didn't like it there. I couldn't help thinking of my mother and how she must have looked after the accident." Later he repressed everything that concerned his mother's death. We see this in the gradual manner in which he recalled the details. Because of this repression, his behaviour grew worse and worse.

We are justified in thinking that the traumatic experience alone was not enough to produce the latent delinquency. The same experience might have made some children neurotic while others would have been untouched. However, we can assume that the psychic trauma was the last of a series of unfavourable experiences dating from early childhood. But we should not assume that the whole etiology of the delinquency is the same as in the traumatic neurosis. In this case, the vagrancy seems to have taken the place of a neurosis; perhaps the boy escaped melancholia in this way. We need more facts for a complete understanding of this delinquency. Whether psychoanalysis could have cured this case we do not know, but it would have disclosed the significant experiences of his childhood and other determining factors. As it is, we must depend on supposition. We can assume that the effect of the mother's accident would not have been so great if the boy had not been so attached to her. It may at first sound paradoxical to speak of delinquency as the result of too great affection. That the boy's relationship to his mother and to his father, also, was very close, we learn from what the boy said. Only two children out of six had survived: the oldest, a sister, fifteen years older, and this boy, who was the youngest. He was the petted one; he slept between his mother and father, the sister on the sofa. After the sister's marriage, when he was twelve, he continued to sleep with his parents. After his father's death, he slept in his father's place, and he began to take care of his mother. This relationship to his mother continued until her death.

We recognize in this boy's conduct an unusually strong identification with the father and a far more than normal relationship to the mother. He had lived with her as if he were the father. I do not mean that this had taken the form of a forbidden relationship. However, in the manner in which he took his mother's death, we have the impression that more than his mother was snatched from him. This abnormal relationship to her could have brought about an emotional disturbance that developed later into delinquency.

We shall have occasion further to see that a too intense early love relationship to parents or to brothers and sisters often leads to delinquency. An affectionate attitude of the child toward members of the family is requisite for normal development. This affection, however, normally should be-

gin to lessen in intensity before puberty, because puberty is
the period in which love objects in the family must be given
up and exchanged for objects outside the family. If the love
relationships within the family are too strong, that is, if a
libidinal fixation has occurred, the way is prepared for
neurosis or for delinquency, as in the case of this boy.

We now take up the case of a delinquent girl of nearly
fourteen, who was sent to the guidance clinic because the
school reported that she was mistreated at home. She was
an orphan and lived with a married uncle, her mother's
brother, who had a small business on the outskirts of the
city. I first interviewed the aunt, who made a not unfavourable impression. It seemed to me that this was probably not
a case of abuse in the usual sense and that it required careful investigation. The aunt complained that the girl, although strong and healthy, did nothing at home but cause
trouble; that she did not appreciate what she and her husband were doing for her. Both parents were dead and the
child would have been entrusted to strangers if her uncle
had not taken her into their home. They had no material interest in taking the child since there was no money for her
care. Her husband had promised the child's mother to take
her. They had done so and had treated her as their own
child. But she would not help with the work at home. When
she came from school, she would just sit around the house,
doing nothing. She had to be forced to do any work at all
and then told constantly to keep at it. She was never on
time for anything; she was stubborn, unreliable, and deceitful. She was so absent-minded that the aunt could not

trust her three-year-old baby to her care for fear something would happen to him. The fact that she showed no grief over the death of her parents indicated how unfeeling she was. She had not cried at their funerals and even now showed no emotion when they were mentioned.

From the description of the child's family, we learned that the father had lived in a small village and had been in good economic circumstances; but that he drank and had tuberculosis. The child had always been well cared for and much loved at home. After the father's death, his wife had sold the business but soon realized that she had made a mistake. She tried to get it back but failed, and because of the strain involved had died six months after her husband. In conclusion, the aunt said that no one could accuse her of abusing her niece although she sometimes lost patience with her. She admitted that she had inflicted corporal punishment on her when her scolding had been in vain but repeated that she had never been cruel to her. The woman told all this in a matter-of-fact way, supported by the conviction that she did not require exoneration.

I then interviewed the girl. She began to talk about school, said that she liked school, that she was fond of her teacher (who had reported the abuse), but that she had very little to do with her schoolmates, and that she had no close friends. She spoke hesitatingly of the home conditions although she knew that a complaint had been made against her aunt and that the summons to the Juvenile Court had been in her interest. She did not mention the corporal punishment; she said, however, that her aunt nagged her a great deal. When I asked her why, she did not answer for a while, then she said, "I have to think so much about my mother and father and how it was at home." At this moment her expression, which had been embarrassed, became distorted, and betrayed the fact that here was a sensitive area. It seemed advisable to follow this lead and I learned that she was so homesick all the time that she had taken refuge in fantasies about her earlier home; that she suffered constantly from a bad dream in which she saw the death-bed of both parents over and over again. She described exactly how her father in the last stages of tuberculosis had begged for water once when she was alone with him, how she handed him the glass, how he drank and had a coughing spell, choked, and fell dead upon the pillow. Although she screamed for help, no one came, and she dared not run away but had to watch the death struggle. Finally her mother came.

On Easter morning a half year later, her mother had sent her to church. As she said good-bye, her mother stood at the window busy with a dust cloth. Hearing a knocking noise which seemed to be made by the dust cloth, she ran back to her mother and took the cloth from her hand to find out what made the noise. She found in it a piece of rope. Because her mother had tried once before to strangle herself to death with a handkerchief, the child took the rope from her mother and threw it away. When she got home from church, she found her dead mother hanging from the crossbar of a window. As she recalled this scene, she behaved in an extraordinary manner. She sat with hands folded to-

gether, her head sunk to one side, and gave herself up to her
thoughts. She seemed to have withdrawn herself completely
from the outside world, and had difficulty in bringing herself back again. When I asked her if she sat this way in her
aunt's home, she answered that often she did not look her
aunt in the face when spoken to, that she turned her head
away as she listened; in this way she could answer without
having to banish her own thoughts. When anyone called to
her loudly, however, it startled her and she found it hard to
come to. When she was left alone to clean the house in the
afternoon, she would lie down on the sofa in a half-lighted
room so that she could dream all the better. Then she would
hear nothing; her aunt said that she often had to knock for
a half hour on the door. She could not trust herself to talk
to her aunt about her day-dreams, but made up all kinds of
excuses which made her seem deceitful. She was not really
dishonest, but no one understood that. Her thoughts came
of themselves and would not be dismissed. But they were not
always terrifying; sometimes they brought her pleasure,
because she could relive happy times in the little village of
her childhood. These memories came with great distinct-
ness; they took possession of her during her work or while
she was playing with the baby or even while she was walking
along the street, especially in the morning when she had
dreamed the night before. They did not come while she was
at school. She did not enjoy the work at home or playing
with the baby because her aunt always blamed her when he
was fretful. She did not complain to her aunt because that
would only make her angry and then there would be quar-

rels which always ended in her aunt's calling her stupid, stubborn, and mean. These statements seemed to me the more credible because to me the child's whole manner was convincing.

In order to round out the picture, I asked for a report from the school. The girl's behaviour in school differed completely from that at home. The grade teacher described her as industrious and attentive, dependable and conscientious about her lessons. She was regarded among her classmates as a pleasing, good-natured girl. She had told only her classmates about the mistreatment at home. They had reported this to the teacher, who had brought the complaint.

We now have the story of the foster mother, the girl, and the school, and in spite of the fullness of the material, we do not yet know what to do. When we compare the statements of the girl and her aunt, we see that this is not a case of mistreatment in the usual sense. At home, the girl seemed to be bad-tempered, obstinate, deceitful, and unwilling to work; in other words, she was dissocial. She admitted this herself, indirectly. On the other hand, her behaviour at school is above reproach. From what we know about delinquency, it is understandable that this foster mother confused the symptoms with the disease and that she tried to cure the dissocial behaviour by eliminating its expression. For the moment, let us not question whether this is delinquency, but assume that it is. This case presents a more difficult problem than that of the boy whose latent delinquency first found expression in running around the streets, and then persisted. In the girl, the latent condition manifests itself only under certain circumstances, at home and not at school. This is confusing, since we know that a psychic trauma usually causes the latent delinquency to become manifest. Although we have such a trauma in the dreadful experience of the death of the two parents, the symptoms appear only in certain situations. There should be an explanation for this.

The symptoms disclose two things: that the girl was tormented by horrible recollections and that she indulged in pleasurable fantasies as well. The latter we designate as day-dreaming. Day-dreaming is doubtless familiar to everyone. All of us have moments in life when we are dissatisfied with the outside world and withdraw into a world of fantasy. In psychoanalytic terms, we say that we take a part of our interest, our libido, away from reality. This libido serves to heighten the significance of our fantasies. This is a normal process so long as our actual relations to the outside world remain undisturbed. A disturbance will result when we take too much libido from the life of reality and use it in a fantasy world. The day-dreams utilize the energy needed in the real world, and make adjustment to reality more difficult. A normal person can banish the most beautiful and compelling fantasies when the tasks of everyday life so demand. Day-dreams can be postponed until favourable moments, when we take a walk or go on a railway journey, or before we go to sleep. Some people are forced into day-dreams when reality becomes unbearable, and cannot free themselves from these fantasies. Psychoanalytically speaking, these people have withdrawn a greater amount of their libido from the outside world than is permissible for health. Such people have practically lost their interest in everyday life; the fantasy world has become the most important thing in life to them. We then have a pathological condition; the total libido is withdrawn from reality.

Let us return to our case. We know that a shocking experience can produce a psychic trauma which will so disturb the psychic mechanisms that, under certain conditions, delinquency will result. This girl did not react to the trauma in the same way as the boy; she was in the process of assimilation of the trauma. The boy succeeded in repressing the trauma; a change of environment had made it possible for him to find an outlet in dissocial behaviour. We cannot explain the difference between the two reactions. We can only assume that the cause lies in certain early childhood experiences. The girl had gone only half-way; the dreadful events had not been forgotten, but had forced themselves back into consciousness as painful recollections. The change of home in her case took her away from people and places familiar and dear to her. She tried to compensate for this deprivation in her day-dreams. It is likely that these fantasies would have enabled her eventually to assimilate the trauma she had suffered. We have seen how this child remained sunk in her fantasies for days, with what difficulty she brought herself back to reality, and how she seemed dissocial in the everyday life of the home. We should be inclined to consider this a severe psychic disturbance if she had not shown a completely different behaviour at school. According to her own statement, she could put the fantasies aside at school and not be disturbed by them.

We now understand the case. This girl was developing a serious psychic illness, which is remote from delinquency. If the day-dreams could not have been stopped, she would have lost all hold on reality and have sunk completely into a fantasy world. The question was how to do this. She herself showed us the way. She behaved normally when she was contented, where she could reproduce a bit of the happy life of her childhood, and could satisfy her need for friendly contacts, as at school. She behaved abnormally at home, where this was impossible. In her aunt's house she was merely tolerated, and instead of being the favoured child, as at home, she was only a nurse-girl to the little cousin. Added to this unpleasantness was the foster mother's complete lack of understanding of the child.

It was impossible to make this woman share our understanding of the case and to change her attitude toward the child. Therefore we had to take the girl out of this home. The foster parents agreed to this, but the question was where to place her. It seemed pointless to put her in another family, since the understanding of the psychic situation in this case is not to be found in the usual foster home. She was placed in an institution where she came under the care of an understanding teacher, who was psychoanalytically trained. She made it possible for the girl to talk about her tragic experiences and thus free herself from their influence. At the same time, she had contact with children of her own age. We assumed that a more congenial environment would help to banish the day-dreams. In the course of a year, she had changed so much that we felt sure she would develop satisfactorily. Although she was not a delinquent, we have made a study of this case for the very reason that illness in a child often gives the appearance of delinquency.

We illustrate further the influence of shocking experiences with two other cases from the institution. The first is a fifteen-year-old girl who had been expelled from school although formerly she had been a reliable, industrious, amenable pupil. The second is a twelve-year-old girl who tried constantly to terrify her schoolmates.

The worker in the first case tried every means possible to solve the difficulty. The more she tried the more annoying and obstinate the girl became, until the worker could no longer keep her in her group. The girl was brought to me for an interview. She began to cry violently, giving no evidence of the cause. Between sobs, she finally told me that she was constantly troubled by the same frightening dream, which in brief was as follows: her mother, already dead, would come to her from the corner of the bedroom, would sit on the edge of her bed, then slowly raise her hand as if to choke her. Every time, just before she was quite dead, she would wake up and could hear herself screaming. After she told me this dream, I asked her how things had been at home, if her mother had always been satisfied with her. She described her home in such a way as to indicate she was the best daughter in the world. The extravagant description of her relationship to her mother made me suspect the opposite. When I asked her if she had never given her mother any trouble, she was noticeably silent. I began talking of other things and then returned to the subject of the mother. She now mentioned that her mother had been bedridden for a long time before her death and added casually that once she had stolen some clothing from her mother. I was not satisfied with the mere mention of this and demanded a more exact account of the theft. The mother was on her death-bed. The girl was standing in front of the house one evening with a girl friend, who suggested there would be no harm in taking some of her mother's clothes. After she was dead, no one would know what she had and they would not be caught. The next morning, the girl was busy cooking when her friend came to get the clothing. It was still in the chest in her mother's room. The girl had not been able to make up her mind to commit the theft and still resisted the temptation of her friend; she did not want to steal. Finally the friend succeeded in banishing her scruples by convincing her how easily it could be accomplished. "You can see the chest from the door. All you have to do is tiptoe in and be careful not to knock anything over; then unlock the chest quietly so that your mother won't hear. Her face is turned to the wall and she won't notice." The girl gave in, and went hesitatingly into the room. The friend stood by the kitchen door and encouraged her with nods as she was about to turn back. She took the key with her, but found that the chest was unlocked. As she opened the chest it made a creaking noise, and in great fright she dropped the key. She was terrified lest her dying mother would turn over and see her. She grabbed what she could reach easily, rushed back to the kitchen, and gave the stolen goods to her friend, who looked on laughing. The friend took the clothing and went away after the two had arranged a meeting for the next day. The friend was to sell the clothing in the meantime. They met the next day but did not divide the spoils. Instead, they decided to go to an amusement park. They rode on the merry-go-round and the Ferris wheel, went to several side-shows, and squandered the rest of the money in a café. They took no thought of the mother at home; on the contrary, they enjoyed themselves. When the girl returned home late, her mother was dead. This did not distress her, but it angered her that relatives were there and scolded her. She was impertinent when they asked her where she had been. She felt no pangs of conscience that she had stolen, not even when suspicion fell on her guardian when it was discovered that the chest had been raided.

These facts came out with great excitement and violent weeping. It was the first time that she had spoken of these things, which had only recently begun to disturb her. She said that the memory of them had become unbearable since her teacher had begun to show some affection for her. She said, "I would have told her long before this but I was afraid she would not like me any more. When she knows how bad I am, she cannot love me." Later the two of us talked with the teacher, who showed great understanding of the situation. The girl, much relieved, went back to her class. She took up her work with new interest, and caused no further trouble. The teacher's task, however, was not finished.

For a while she spent a little time each evening with the
girl before she went to bed. She encouraged her to talk
about her dead mother. The girl finally came to understand
that it was her great guilt which made her feel unworthy of
the teacher's love. Her fear of the old dream became less
and finally disappeared. By means of an identification
with the teacher, she came to have a more normal attitude
toward life.

The second case is the girl who tried to terrify her classmates. It was noteworthy that this child chose for this purpose only red material which she made into masks and head-
dresses. She had a passion for all kinds of red material and
developed a great cleverness in securing them. She employed whatever she could lay her hands on in this fashion:
paper, cloth, ribbon, etc. It required some time to discover
the cause of this behaviour. First we learned that she had
been severely frightened while she was still in the first
grade. On Krampus Day,[3] in the evening, she went out on
an errand for her mother, and on the stairway in the half
darkness she met someone wearing a red mask, disguised as
Krampus. In her first terror, she went running back to the
apartment. But the Krampus ran after her, struck her with
his switch, and followed her into the room, chasing her
under the bed! The child remembered still how he pulled
her out from under the bed. What happened after that, she
could not recall. This story was reproduced with great af-

---

[3] Krampus is a character of Austrian folk-lore who looks like a devil
and carries a bundle of switches. He comes on December 6 as a forewarn-
ing to children to be good so that they will receive presents at Christmas.

fect, but it brought no change in the child's behaviour. It was only after we discovered an earlier experience that we had any success. When she was four years old, she had been taken by her mother to see a woman with red hair. We could establish the accuracy of her age at this time since the event occurred shortly before the separation of the parents. During the visit, a fight had ensued in which the mother pulled the other woman's hair down. Meanwhile the child, standing near her mother, was knocked over, injured, and her face began to bleed. Both the mother and the child were thrown out of the house. The child's last impression of the scene was the woman's bloody face surrounded by red hair. When they got home, the father and the mother had a fight. The child recalled that this was the last time she had seen her father. This quarrel between the wife and the husband's mistress was followed by the separation of the parents.

We cannot now undertake an explanation of why the child wished to terrify others as she herself had been terrified. An understanding of the deeper motives of this behaviour requires further study. At this point, we have only to recognize that shocking experiences can lead to psychic traumas and thence to delinquency.

FOUR

SOME CAUSES OF DELINQUENCY

(CONTINUED)

ALTHOUGH we must guard against generalization, our study of several cases seems to justify the formulation of a general principle. Delinquency represents one of the departures from the normal in psychic processes, and for this reason a solution of the problem of delinquency depends on understanding the psychic content. Since we have learned to think psychoanalytically, we know that dissocial behaviour is the result of disturbed psychic patterns, of abnormal accumulation of affect. The manner in which the psychic energy is utilized determines the direction in which the individual develops; whether he will be psychically normal, whether he will be subjected to nervous illness, or whether he will become dissocial.

Since our explanations and conclusions up until now seem obvious, you may underestimate the necessity for a thorough study of psychoanalysis. You may even believe that you can simply adopt a few psychoanalytic principles and carry on your work as formerly. Such an idea would lead you into dilettantism, which is more dangerous than complete ignorance. Not every delinquent is an interesting psychoanalytic or neurotic problem, but there are so many possible determinants for every delinquent act that our investigation must be guided by sound theoretical knowledge. I do not wish to alarm you, but simply to warn you that unless we avoid all haste and superficiality, we are doomed to failure.

The next case is that of an eighteen-year-old boy brought to me by the mother. My first advice was that the child should be examined by a psychiatrist. The doctors were unable to find any sign of nervous disorder and attributed the laziness and aggressive behaviour of which the mother complained to a conflict within the family. The mother was a widow; the father, who had been foreman in a large factory, had died many years before. After his death, the mother secured an office position which barely sufficed to support herself and the children. The situation had been better during the past year since the oldest daughter had begun to work. She was a year younger than our patient, had learned the trade of seamstress, and was employed in a dressmaking shop. There were three more children in the family: girls, aged fifteen, thirteen, and ten years.

When the mother returned with her son after the doctors' examination, I asked her to wait while I interviewed the boy alone. The boy made a feminine impression; he seemed shy and ill at ease, and was at first uncommunicative. It was hard to believe that this boy was capable of the aggressive acts ascribed to him, and I realized at once that they must be momentary outbursts of affect rather than the expression of a brutal nature. I learned the following important facts during the long interview with the boy. He had completed the seventh grade of the public school with a creditable record. His plan to continue his work in high school was interrupted by the death of his father. He wanted to apprentice himself to a painter, but since he could find no opening, he had taken the job of errand-boy in a drug store about December of the same year. Because of his mother's eagerness to have him learn a trade, he gave up this job after a few weeks and apprenticed himself to a carpenter. He liked this job and remained over a year until he discovered that his employer was not a master carpenter and therefore had no right to train apprentices. He was so much annoyed by this that for some time he refused to enter another carpenter shop. Finally, however, he secured another apprenticeship through his mother. He lost this job nine months later because the firm went bankrupt. By this time he had had enough of carpentry. His mother tried everything from kind words to beating to make him change his mind, but to no avail. He had no further interest in learning a trade, and after weeks of job-hunting became an errand-boy again, this time in a paper store. He was discharged after six weeks because he refused to carry out an order which was offensive to him. A relative now took him in charge because his mother would have nothing more to do with him. He left home to become an apprentice in a planing mill, but returned after eight weeks. Previously there had been only short intervals between jobs, but this time he remained unemployed for half a year. He was brought to me after he had failed to hold his last job, as errand-boy in a dry-goods house.

The boy declared that he did not want to be a burden to his mother since he was strong and healthy, but he refused to become a common labourer as his mother wished. He would be content to learn carpentry if he could be given credit for his first year's apprenticeship, but nobody was willing to straighten out this affair. During the time he was unemployed, he had enjoyed helping his mother with the housework. He especially liked washing dishes and house-cleaning. He read a lot in his spare time—anything that came to his hand, without discrimination. He became excited when we discussed his relationship to the different members of the family. He seemed especially to hate his oldest sister. I learned that his fits of anger were chiefly directed against her. He felt insulted because his sisters belittled him and laughed at him. The oldest sister was the leader in this, and his mother, instead of standing up for him, took the side of the girls. He explained to me with considerable affect that the boy in a family ought to have a say as well as the girls. He liked his mother best, and the sisters in the order of their age, the youngest first. He could not bear his oldest sister because she was always disagreeable and wanted to boss everything. The sisters were quite different in appearance. The oldest was taller than he, had a narrow face, blue eyes, and blond hair. She resembled the mother, but the other sisters looked more like their father. The mother and sisters were very religious, but he had liberal socialistic views, which he had never discussed with his family. They associated only with strict Catholics. They took him to social gatherings with them without knowing how repugnant this was to him. He did not dare tell his mother of the conflict about the difference in their ideas. He liked to visit one of his mother's friends because he met a girl there whom he admired very much although the rest of the people were uncongenial. He was embarrassed when I asked him whether he had ever liked any girls before, but then admitted that at thirteen he had been in love with one of his oldest sister's schoolmates who spent a great deal of time with them. He remembered her as similar in appearance to his sister except that her hair was a deeper blond, and her eyes grey-blue. When I asked him whether he was in love at the moment, he blushed, but then spoke with enthusiasm of the girl already mentioned. Had he ever kissed her? "A boy doesn't do that," he replied, flushing and embarrassed. His description of her made her in every way the older sister's opposite, although he seemed unaware of this fact. She had black hair and dark-brown eyes. When I asked whether he knew anyone in his childhood with such eyes and hair, he mentioned his youngest sister. Questioned about his childhood, he gave several recollections. The first was about "saying pieces" on holidays, an important custom in the family. One time when he was very little, he and his oldest sister had competed in reciting birthday greetings. The father had promised a picture book to the one who recited best. She got the prize, and he was so angry that he tore up the book. The narrative sequence of this incident was reversed in his memory; he began by describing how his father had whipped him for his naughtiness. He also told me that he and this sister had loved to play father and mother as children, and that the youngest sister was always their child in this game.

This ended our interview and I called the mother in. She was irritated that she had been kept waiting, and immediately told me that she could not understand why I had to talk so long to the boy because I knew already what the trouble was; she had told me that at our first meeting before I sent her to the clinic. It was obvious that she felt her authority as mother threatened. She was a lean woman of middle height with sharp features and hard eyes. She gave the impression of being an energetic person whom nothing could daunt. Life had treated her badly from childhood. Although married life had given her material security, she had not had a satisfactory relationship with her husband. After his death it had been a struggle to maintain the five children. Her oldest daughter was an exceptional girl who turned over all her earnings to the mother. With her help they could have got along much better if it had not been for the trouble with the boy. The mother felt that her husband never understood the deeper needs of her nature. He was a cheerful person who took life lightly; he was undiscriminating in all his pleasures, including women. There were no open quarrels between them, but the wife withdrew more and more from her husband. "I always had to stand apart from life. My religious upbringing was very strict. When I later discovered how much these principles were contradicted by actual life, I suffered for years until I finally reached a solution within myself." She spoke of her son in a deprecating way as though he no longer meant anything to her. "He is not a man, just a stupid, stubborn boy who thinks he knows it all. He tries to lord it over his sisters, and naturally they won't stand for it. He carries on so and talks so foolishly that the girls laugh at him; this makes him furious and he attacks them like a wild animal, especially the oldest. If I don't get him out of the house, something terrible is bound to happen. He obeys me; he doesn't dare defy me because he knows that I would whip him even though he is eighteen years old. He acts like a child. After he has been up to something, he is very obedient and clears up everything around the house nicely. He is a very orderly boy; his closet is much neater than any of his sisters', and he gets mad if they disturb anything. On the other hand, he is careless about his person. I have to make sure that his neck and ears are clean. But he will stand before the mirror for an hour arranging his tie and combing his hair. Of course his sisters are annoyed by this. He thinks only of himself. In the morning he won't get up and doesn't clean his shoes. He has no initiative; housework and reading books are no work for a grown boy; he ought to have a steady job. I won't support him any longer. I haven't the money and he has to learn that we won't slave for him. He is not even honest; when I send him to the store, he cheats me in small amounts, which he spends on candy like a school child. I refuse to bear it any longer; he has to take work as a labourer and earn his own bread and butter."

We feel that the mother's complaints are to some extent justified and that she is wise in seeking help in this intolerable situation. What is to be done? Perhaps you think that having heard both sides, we should now bring mother and son together and try to find a middle road out of the difficulty, encourage one or the other, urge them to be more patient and so try to reach a compromise. *Such a type of procedure would be as ineffectual as a moral lecture about delinquency.* It is not our job to make peace, nor to judge the boy, but rather to solve the problem. We know that we must first discover the cause of the dissocial behaviour by understanding the psychic situation which produced it. For the moment it is only the emotional reactions of this dissocial boy which interest us, and therefore we must examine the facts for their subjective rather than objective validity. Everything we learn about the case must contribute to this. This implies that we take the side of the boy. Since we believe that all psychic manifestations are somehow predetermined, we must say to ourselves, "He is in the right, there must be reasons for this behaviour." What would we gain by being shocked, or by joining the ranks of those who are distressed by his behaviour? Moral or ethical condemnation will not help us.

The most disagreeable of the boy's traits, his brutality at home and especially that toward the oldest sister, should be our first interest. We eliminate all moral judgments and see the brutality for what it is, the manifestation of a long latent situation. Dynamically this could be expressed by saying that the discharge of psychic energy no longer remains within social bonds. This trait might be constitutionally determined. If we believed this, it would concern us no further; his laziness would be the only problem left for us to deal with. But this can hardly be a case of constitutional brutality since nothing about the boy corresponds to the type—neither the impression he made on me nor the description supplied by the mother. What the boy said made us feel that his aggressions were momentary outbreaks of affect, and as such they deserve our interest. We find aggression directed chiefly against the oldest sister and we have further evidence that he hates her. One of his childhood memories might indicate a source of this hate. As a very small boy, he probably experienced very painful slights. You will remember the story about the birthday book. Experience in the treatment of neurotics by psychoanalysis has taught us that such a memory usually serves as the façade for many other similar memories which are recalled in the course of treatment. We see that this father was tactless in his treatment of the boy, that he disregarded his feelings and apparently did not understand him. It seems probable, too, that there was actual favouritism shown the little girl by the father. We might therefore say that the boy's dislike of his several sisters was founded on the slights endured as a child, and that he particularly hated the oldest sister because she was her father's favourite. The constellation in this family is one we frequently encounter. The father prefers the daughters to the

son, the mother has no special need for affection, and the
son is therefore cheated. The same can be true of girls if the
situation is reversed.

At this point a few general statements are pertinent.
Anyone who has contact with children, whether as parent
or teacher, will find himself continually faced with a phenomenon which no effort on his part can quite eliminate.
The harmony of every nursery is continually disturbed by
feelings of envy and jealousy within the group, though the
parents try to avoid any show of favouritism. Observation
should have taught us what psychoanalysis has to say on
this subject, i. e., that every child regards his brothers and
sisters as competitors in the struggle for the important
first place in the love of the parents. This rivalry does not
endanger the child's development if parents deal sensibly
with each situation as it comes. Many mothers do the right
thing by instinct; others make continual mistakes without
realizing it. In these cases it often happens that the relationship between brothers and sisters lacks warmth even in
later life. The more unfavourable the circumstances the
greater the likelihood that they will lead to delinquency.
The situation of this boy must have been thoroughly unfavourable. In addition to an unsympathetic father he had a
clever but hard woman as a mother. Nevertheless we cannot
accept his suffering from lack of love as the cause of his delinquency. Why not? Because the other incident which he
related about his childhood makes this theory untenable.

We heard that the sister he now hated had at one time
been his favourite playmate. This would have been impos-

sible had they been bitter rivals. We might suppose that the relationship had been ambivalent were it not that they played mother and father, with the youngest sister as their child. Of course we do not know how long this relationship between the children lasted, but we are safe in supposing that countless other memories similar in character lie behind the one he told us. Can this fact help us to find a cause for his delinquency? We might set up as a premise the supposition that his hate of his sister was determined by an unconscious erotic tie to her. Because of your lack of familiarity with psychoanalysis, it may sound fantastic to hear talk of an erotic tie where only violent hate manifests itself. If our supposition were founded only on the childhood memory it would have little justification. There are other facts, however, which support this. You may wonder that we should proceed on such a doubtful assumption, especially since psychoanalytic experience teaches us that the first statements of a patient are often altered or refuted by the deeper material which is disclosed later in the analysis. But do not forget that our work differs from that of the psychoanalyst. We are not in the position of being able to wait; because we must act quickly, we are forced to form a picture of a situation after a few interviews. We know that our conclusions are no more than partly right, and that only the result of the treatment will show how far our assumptions were correct. We can lessen the uncertainty by a careful study of the material at our command.

Before returning to the case under discussion, we should make clear what we mean by "erotic tie." We are justified in supposing that the brother and sister shared an intense experience while playing the game of father and mother. We know that this childish game is not always harmless, that children put more into it than is commonly supposed, and that playing husband and wife frequently ends with examining each other's bodies and thus satisfying childish curiosity. We have often found in our practice that children act out in these games what they have observed their parents doing. Under crowded living conditions, it frequently happens that children have the opportunity to see sexual intercourse between their parents. Certainly such games are a source of excitement which can only be termed sexual, although this word is used in a broader sense than usual. The memories which survive these experiences serve to bind the partners strongly to each other, and the more intense the emotion the stronger the tie. Even though he is not caught in the act, the child is certain to learn that what he did and felt on these occasions was wrong. He understands the difference between these games which he invents for his own pleasure and those which are approved. If the drive toward the instinctual pleasure remains stronger than his fear of punishment, the games are continued; if the other impulse conquers, the experience is repressed. Children at this age are not capable of solving the conflict consciously by rejecting the forbidden pleasure. They try therefore to forget the game and everything associated with it, including the feelings for the partner involved, which represent the greatest danger to renewed temptation. Repression cuts these impulses off from this form of expression, but they continue to exist in the unconscious. After conscious control has been lost, these impulses are subjected to the influence of other forces in the unconscious and the result is what psychoanalysis calls a fixation. We can easily understand that the ties to the child partner are not broken but simply displaced, i. e., an unconscious erotic tie is formed. The danger of this attachment becoming conscious is lessened if the feeling is completely reversed, if the love relationship finds conscious expression as hate. We now have a general conception of what we mean by an unconscious erotic tie, although it is hardly possible to grasp the full significance of this psychoanalytic principle at once. In the case of our patient, we lack proof that the boy's hate for his sister was so determined. If we say that it could have developed out of their childish game, we draw an analogy with the neurotic. But our boy is a delinquent and not a neurotic. We must therefore find other material to strengthen our supposition. I believe it will be helpful to discuss another theory before returning to the facts of the case.

You are familiar with the term "puberty." The common belief is that it refers only to the physiological changes, the maturing of the genital organs in both sexes which takes place during this period. But many individuals are unable to fulfil the function of reproduction in spite of having normally developed sexual organs. They are incapable of feeling the necessary attraction for persons of the opposite sex, or else their psychic constitution is such that it demands other than normal sexual gratification. Freud has

shown us that an understanding of puberty is impossible
unless the psychological component is considered. He has
deepened our insight into that psychic development which
normally ends with adolescence and has studied the results
of disturbances at various points. One fact is of immediate
importance to us: that at adolescence the youth should give
up his first love objects within the family and replace them
by others outside this circle. In psychoanalytic terms, the
infantile libidinal ties must be loosened in order to free the
libido for object relationships outside of the family. If the
libidinal ties to the infantile objects are too strong, are
fixated, it becomes difficult or impossible to loosen them in
puberty.

Our boy's relationship to the opposite sex indicates that
he has been only partially successful in accomplishing this
task of puberty. Such a failure results from an infantile
fixation on some member of the family. It is not normal for
an eighteen-year-old boy to say "a boy doesn't do that"
when asked if he has ever kissed a girl. We may consider
that this strengthens our argument. The boy's statements
about his love object deserve our interest. The first girl
whom he loved at the age of thirteen was the same age as his
oldest sister, her friend and classmate. The two differed little in manner and in appearance. His love object is here
still, the sister, and yet not the sister herself. His present
love object has nothing in common with the sister except
her work; in appearance, she is her opposite in every detail. Does this tell us anything? We know that as the result

of repression of the forbidden childish game, everything associated with it is likewise repressed; also that because the love tie to the partner in the game is not really loosened, there is constant danger of its reappearance in reality. The great surge of libido which comes at puberty makes the boy for the first time able to carry out his sexual desires and increases the danger that the sister may become the object of these desires. This danger is lessened if conscious hate blocks the approach to her. It is now possible to understand why the repressed libido had to be changed to hate. The process was accomplished by one of the repressing tendencies which protects the ego. The conscious hate acts as a safety measure and must remain as long as the unconscious erotic tie exists, to prevent its breaking through from the unconscious. It remains a question whether any other tendency was operative to make him give up the sister as sexual object.

Freud has taught us that the surge of libido in puberty is accompanied by a strong wave of repression. This is more powerful in girls than in boys, but in both cases it encounters the early love objects and excludes them as sexual objects. Psychoanalysis says that the incest barrier is erected. The statements of the boy in this case indicate how effective was the repression. We can actually see how this barrier began to raise itself when at thirteen he exchanged his sister for the girl similar to her. His present love choice is even more illuminating. The incest barrier has been extended to the type represented by the sister, making the type sexually unapproachable. Yet the youth has not departed from the family. His last love object resembles the youngest sister to whom he is bound by a weaker tie.

Let us formulate our findings in order not to lose perspective. We are discussing an eighteen-year-old boy who is accused of aggressive behaviour at home, especially toward his oldest sister. Our first idea had to be rejected, that the favouritism shown the eldest daughter and the neglect he experienced in childhood led to his dissocial behaviour. A memory which he tells of his childhood leads us to believe that this aggression was determined by an unconscious erotic tie to the sister. We were led to this assumption because of the analogous condition to be found in the neurotic, but we found significant facts to confirm it; first, the evidence that the patient's relation to the opposite sex was considerably inhibited, and second the fact that he chose a love object in every way his sister's opposite. I selected this case to present to you because it illustrates many important points in our method of treatment. It shows how deeply we probe for the determining cause of delinquency and how we follow every given clue without waiting for the child to work with us. Our procedure is to set up a picture of the case which will serve to reduce the inevitable element of uncertainty. If you recall that establishing the cause of delinquency was found equivalent to discovering the conditions which had led to latent delinquency, you will understand that we have already fulfilled a part of our purpose. An unconscious erotic tie is one of the psychic conditions that build up a mechanism requiring only a provocation to set it in motion.

Let us now continue our inquiry and consider a remark which the mother made about her son. "He is not a man, just a stupid, stubborn boy." Does this tell us anything? We should compare it with, "He obeys me; he doesn't dare defy me because he knows that I would whip him even though he is eighteen years old. . . . After he has been up to something, he is very obedient and clears up everything around the house nicely." We are inclined to agree that he is not a man; he certainly does not act like one. But does he fit the description of a stupid, stubborn boy? His actions point in another direction. He does the work about the house usually done by the women. He makes no protest against this; in fact he enjoys it. His closet is neater than those of his sisters; he stands before the mirror for hours brushing his hair and arranging his tie; he is shy and fearful like a girl. In short, he shows many feminine traits which accord with his appearance. This may be an inherent factor, added to which is the experience of growing up without a father and surrounded only by women. He made no mention of other boys; he spoke only of his sisters and their friends. It often happens that men brought up in a strictly feminine environment develop feminine traits. The fact is unmistakable in this youth. We recognize it not only in his own statements and in what his mother tells us, but we also see it clearly in his whole personality. It is this feminine streak in her son which the mother resents and which causes

the boy conflict when he tries to assert his masculinity. This
conflict, which vents itself in outbursts of affect, we may
consider the second determinant of his behaviour. Are we
right in this? Again we must turn to psychoanalysis for
deeper insight. We have already learned about identifications, that they are the product of the early attachment of
the child to his parents and that if this attachment becomes
too strong it will lead to an abnormal development or to
delinquency. In order to understand this, we should study
the normal psychic development. It will simplify the presentation to discuss the development in the male child only
and to assume that that of the girl is analogous.

The parents are generally the first persons to enter the
sphere of the child's experience, and for this reason the
child's first feelings are directed toward them. At first the
libidinal strivings of the child are directed equally toward
mother and father; the child loves both equally. In the
course of time the feelings for his mother increase, and although he continues to love his father, situations arise
which make the father objectionable. Even a three-year-old
child can so resent his father's tenderness toward his mother
that he would like to get rid of him so that he can have his
mother to himself. His feelings for his father now vary;
love is at times replaced by rejection. Psychoanalysis de-
scribes this as an ambivalent attitude toward the father.
The name chosen by Freud to characterize this unmistakable stage of development has often been misinter-
preted. He calls it the Œdipus stage, making reference to
the classic myth. You will remember that Œdipus married

his mother after killing his father, although neither mother nor son knew of their kinship. Those people who do not wish to understand the psychoanalytic way of thinking raise a cry of indignation at the idea of comparing the relationship between Œdipus and his mother with that of the little boy to his mother. But you who want to understand deserve an explanation. The little boy can no more actually kill his father than he can think of having sexual relations with his mother; his sexual apparatus is too immature. The name "Œdipus situation" only signifies the same tendency translated into the emotions of this stage of development, for which the child cannot be held accountable. In psychoanalysis the word "sexual" has come to have a much broader and deeper meaning than was previously the case. As the child's development continues, this negative feeling for his father conflicts with the positive feelings, and is therefore repressed. The real Œdipus situation becomes the Œdipus complex, with all of its repercussions from the unconscious. If no further disturbances occur, the Œdipus complex is resolved approximately at the beginning of the sixth year. Its resolution marks the time of identification with the parents. The positive Œdipus complex is formed out of the tender relationship to the mother; the negative out of the similar relationship to the father. The first results in a positive attitude toward the mother and a negative attitude toward the father. The second is positive toward the father and negative toward the mother. The positive feelings from both these sources, which in every individual are variously coloured by the negative, unite to

form a father-and-mother identification. As the growth
process continues, these identifications result in a gradual
assimilation of the characteristics of the two parents. If the
development is not normal—if, for example, the identification with the mother becomes too strong as a result of hereditary or of environmental factors, the boy will acquire fe-
male traits and his character will become feminine. The
stronger the mother identification becomes, the more the
father identification is impaired, and in corresponding
measure, all masculine tendencies. The boy grows up de-
ficient in manliness, and his adolescence is prolonged on this
account.

This fact had catastrophic importance for the boy in our
case. His father died just as he was finishing school at the
age of fourteen. Since he was the oldest child and the only
man in the family, he was faced with the task of taking his
father's place. Had he been a normally developed boy, he
would have been able to do this. But the father identification, which external circumstances forced on him, failed
time and again. His mother told us, "He tries to lord it
over his sisters, and naturally they won't stand for it.
He carries on so and talks so foolishly that the girls laugh
at him; this makes him furious and he attacks them like a
wild animal." He himself declared with great affect that he
was "somebody" and that not only the girls had the say in
a household. His inability to act like a man caused him conflict, which he tried to master by excessive brutality. His
sisters sensed that he was a cowering woman rather than a
forceful man, and made fun of him until he was beside him-

self with anger. We now have a second explanation for his aggressions. This lack of success in the father identification is clearly the result of his identification with his mother.

But still another conflict disturbed him and helped to determine his behaviour. This was the clash of his own socialistic philosophy of life with the strict Catholic ideas of his family. He refused to see any good in their religion, rejected it completely for himself, and yet was too weak to oppose his mother. Instead, he never mentioned the subject, so that his mother was unaware of his real opinion. This resentment also found release in his aggressive behaviour. After each outbreak, he gave in and kept on submitting to the mother's authority. In only one thing was his opposition unwavering: he would not become a common labourer. This resistance was reinforced by his determination to show the girl he was fond of that he was worth something. To be a common labourer was to be nothing, and as long as he escaped this destiny, there still remained a chance for him to prove his worth. We have gone as far in disclosing the determinants of the aggressions of this boy as is necessary before beginning treatment. We now see that the laziness about which we were consulted is not real laziness. The boy's unfortunate experiences and the opposition of his family have put him in a desperate position. If a change could be brought about in his relationship to his mother and sisters, and if he could find suitable work, it seemed likely that a great improvement would result.

Let us now consider methods of treatment. Above all it

seemed important that the boy be spared further experience of failure in the father identification. An easy way to accomplish this was for me to take over the father role in this family for a time. If the boy acknowledged me as the father, he would no longer have to play the part, and one of his conflict situations would be eliminated. With my help he should be able to attain a better relationship with the members of his family. But I would accomplish more if I could bring them into the proper transference relationship to me. The knowledge that I was there, ready to act with father authority if need arose, should change their attitude toward their brother, and the relationship would be improved on both sides. In the same way, the harassed mother would be relieved of anxiety and therefore would be able to adopt a more reasonable attitude toward her son. This is a superficial description of what takes place in the external situation when the worker steps in to fill the father role in the family. Such external change is all we strive for in the beginning. I did not mention my purpose. The first interview offered possibilities for creating the proper transference. The boy responded at once when he felt that he was talking to someone who really understood his misery. The opportunity given her to unburden herself by talking was important in the case of the mother; she left with the feeling of having found someone who could and would help her. She was easily dissuaded from her plan to force the boy out of the house to seek work as a labourer. I was able to arrange that he be given credit for his first year of apprenticeship and go on with learning carpentry. He began work two weeks after our first meeting, and did well. He gave no indication of laziness. We settled the conflict about religion by talking the matter over with his mother. In my presence, the mother promised to allow her son perfect freedom in this respect. After that he no longer joined the family in their social gatherings except when he had the opportunity to meet the girl mentioned earlier.

Doubtless you expect me to tell you the plan that I made for clearing up all his dissocial behaviour. But I confess that I am unable to do this, nor am I certain that it would be possible in any case. It has been my practice for years to utilize favourable situations, or, if none exist, to create them; intuition and deliberation serve me alternately, depending on the case. This may seem a very uncertain method, but it may be that ties exist between the unconscious of the analysed worker and the unconscious of his patient which ensure the accuracy of the work.

It may interest you to hear how the boy reacted during the early part of the treatment. When alone with me, he would scold about his sisters; when we were all together, he played the part of the superior older brother, would look at me with a meaningful nod to see whether I observed how silly the girls were. Peace was restored to the family at the end of a few weeks. The change in atmosphere reacted favourably on each member of the group, although no single member recognized what part he played in bringing this about. The mother's opinion, when asked how things were going, was "much better, he now behaves much more sensibly." The boy attributed the change to the fact that his oldest sister was less disagreeable and that his mother now took his part. I had given the mother some understanding of the boy's conflict, and her changed attitude made the boy feel that she was on his side. For four months I saw the boy two or three times a week, usually not at home. We discussed his aggressive behaviour with the result that he came to understand its meaning. At first the outbreaks continued, although they were not so violent as before. They calmed down gradually, and during the last two months of treatment completely disappeared. In this case, the cure was permanent.

FIVE

UNDERLYING CAUSES
OF DELINQUENCY

WE do not always have to go so deeply into our problem to discover the original causes of dissocial outbreaks as was necessary in the cases described in the last chapter. Nor do we always need to uncover these first causes before we start our work of re-education. It suffices at first to make sure of the direction in which they lie. The course of the treatment will of itself lead us into the deeper underlying causes of the delinquency.

I shall now tell you about a boy in our institution whose difficulties became clear after a single interview because of our psychoanalytic understanding. However, I shall not try at the present time to differentiate between the immediate precipitating cause and the deeper motives. My intention is to show you how the psychoanalytically trained worker looks at the situation, and how he draws his conclusions.

From the case history, we learned that the boy was a seventeen-year-old carpenter's helper, and had been learning his trade in his father's shop. Here he had repeatedly stolen considerable amounts of denatured alcohol and some lumber. The father had first tried threats and then severity, entirely without effect. The parents were troubled about him and hoped a period in our institution would influence him for the better.

I was struck by the statement in the history that he had urinated into the empty bottles in order to conceal the theft of the denatured alcohol. We could pass over this point as something accidental, and be satisfied with the explanation that it was easy for him to cover up the theft in this way since urine has the same colour as denatured alcohol. But let us look for other possible reasons. Why did he do just this? We need the knowledge that we have gained from psychoanalysis to help us answer this question. While reading the history, I recalled the analysis of a neurotic patient in which there had been a similar situation, where the act of urinating into a bottle had meant revenge on his father, carried out by the same organ with which he felt his father had injured him. It occurred to me that this action might have the same meaning for this dissocial boy. Perhaps I have aroused your antagonism with this assumption and you may repudiate this explanation as absurd or unacceptable. But you must suspend judgment and consider the facts. When you learn to look at things differently you will not raise immediate objections but will say that perhaps it could be so. We do not yet know whether our assumption is true or not; we must first observe the boy in the institution and talk with him.

A much more important and serious argument against the interpretation of single incidents like this is the danger of drawing too general conclusions from them. If we try to spare ourselves a thorough examination of the boy himself we shall go astray; we may easily overlook facts and arrive at false conclusions. We must approach the situation without prejudice and preconceived ideas, and consider carefully all that he has to say It was only a fortunate coincidence that enabled me, through my experience with the neurotic case, to gain a clue to the significance of this boy's behaviour.

When this boy came, a big, husky, overgrown youth, I received him myself, as I did all newly admitted boys. After this I had no direct contact with him for a period in which I left him to adjust himself to the environment. The reasons for this mode of procedure will be clearer when we discuss the subject of the relationship which must be established between the child and the worker or counsellor. About two weeks after the boy's admission, a nice-looking young woman of about twenty-five came to ask about him. Up to this time, I had not yet had a long talk with him. However, I had kept in touch with the people in contact with him and I knew what he was doing. I took it for granted that the girl was his sister and was surprised to find that she was his stepmother. From his counsellor I learned that he often talked of his stepmother in his group and had already written her two letters. I had no idea of their content as we did not read our charges' letters, and they could write when and to whom they pleased. The woman was willing to talk freely about her stepson, and spoke understandingly about him in spite of all the difficulties he had made at home. When she told me how the neighbours held her responsible for the behaviour of the boy—because that is always the

way with stepmothers—she cried and got very much excited that she should be so blamed. She said that she was
not a bad stepmother, that she treated the boy well, that
he would say so too, because he liked her. When I asked
her how she knew that he liked her so much, she became
embarrassed and hesitated. When I pressed her for an answer, she said that it would be so easy for me to misunderstand and that I might suspect something for which there
were no grounds. I assured her that I would think nothing
of the sort, that I would listen attentively and that her co-
operation would be very important for the real understanding of the boy. Thereupon she related: "When we go along
the street together he often turns to me and says, 'See,
Mother, how people look at us.' That makes me think that
he considers himself a grown-up man. He has written me
twice to come to visit him and in both letters he asked me
to wear my brown dress so that the boys could see it." I
asked her if she had the dress on. "Yes, I must give him
some pleasure." We talked of other things, of her relationship to the boy and to his father, which seemed throughout
normal and pleasant. Returning to the subject of her relationship to the boy, she said that he had often told her
to let him know when she needed money and then he would
sell his father's lumber and bring the money to her. She
had never taken any from him and had not known of the
actual stealing for a long time. She had always felt that
this talk was only joking. It was she, however, who first
learned of his misdemeanours. All her efforts to influence
him for the better were in vain so that she finally decided

to tell his father. He was unable to influence the boy either with mildness or severity. The boy became more troublesome and more hostile toward his father. Because of the stealing, they were afraid to try to get him another job. It therefore seemed necessary to place him in an institution. The woman became gradually more confidential and said spontaneously that she had always felt that the boy had more feeling for her than children usually have for a stepmother. For this reason she could not understand why he did not change his behaviour in response to her admonitions, and she came to doubt his real feeling for her. There had been no question of a more intimate relationship between them. I felt certain of this not only from my impression of the woman herself but also because of the way in which she gave this information. She had been married to the boy's father for three years. She was a friend of his mother, and long before her death had been a frequent visitor in the house. The boy was twelve when her friendship with his mother began. Even at that time she had found him an alert, pleasing boy who often showed her a kind of childish tenderness.

We can easily imagine the conflict into which this boy was thrown. During his adolescence a woman appears in the household who is not enough older to be excluded as a love object. He directs his libidinal strivings toward her. The relationship goes on peacefully for two years; nothing improper happens; he has for her the normal tender feelings of an adolescent. We can assume that had his mother lived, this woman, who later became his stepmother, would have been only one stage in his development; but the father marries her when she was still an object of adoration to the boy. He is at puberty, a period in which the unconscious erotic feelings can come very close to breaking through into consciousness. Such erotic expressions were now no longer permissible and must be repressed. This brought the boy into an unbearable relationship to his father. The father had not only taken the loved one away from his son, but now forces her on him as a mother. This aroused hate and aggression against the father. Thus the dissocial behaviour of the boy becomes understandable. It is analogous to the neurotic symptom which has its motivation in unconscious sexual wishes.

The neighbours were right. The stepmother was a cause of the boy's misdemeanours, but not in the way they thought and not in a sense which she and the boy could comprehend.

We shall conclude the discussion of the causes of dissocial behaviour here and take up other questions of remedial training, breaking away from the usual procedure of interpolating theoretical explanations. I shall now give a continuous report of a case from the time the boy was brought to me to the point at which we might consider him adjusted. The theoretical considerations in this case we shall leave to the end. We shall not concern ourselves too deeply with the causes of the delinquency but shall consider more in detail the process of treatment.

A factory foreman brought his seventeen-year-old son into the child-guidance clinic because he wanted to put him in an institution. The boy was at this time apprenticed to a shoemaker. From the father we learned certain important facts. Until the previous summer the son had been a good boy who made no trouble at home or in the shop. One day he asked his father for some money, saying that he could get the leather to make himself a pair of shoes cheap. He obtained the money but failed to come home that night, and the family learned the next day that he had not been at the shop. Since such a thing had never happened before, the family was very much concerned, feared that he had met with an accident or had been attacked. They reported his disappearance to the police and inquired about him daily at headquarters. Six days later his mother received word that he had been picked up penniless by the police in another city and was already on his way home. The family was overjoyed at his return, but this pleasure was soon forgotten in the distress over his subsequent behaviour. The boy would not talk. He refused to tell his father why he had left his work or where he had spent the week. He became more obdurate and defiant, and would say nothing more than that he had been to Graz, the city in which he had been picked up. His father became excited, a great scene occurred, and finally he gave his son a severe beating. After this things went from bad to worse. The boy would not work, stayed away from home, hung about the streets or in cafés all day, and stayed out later and later at night. As if this were not enough, he continued to get money out of his father and his employer. His father punished him with increasing severity in the hope of changing his behaviour. Since this only made him worse and drove him further from his family, his mother began to take his part and persuaded her husband to be more gentle with him. This method brought only temporary improvement, and finally his mother's patience was exhausted and his father reverted once more to force. Severity and kindness were tried alternately several times, but the boy only acted worse. The father concluded his remarks to me with the following words: "You can't imagine how awful it is. We've tried to be good to him and we've tried being strict and beating him, but nothing helps. We don't know what to do next. Perhaps if he goes into an institution, they can make something out of him."

Up to this point the father had confined his talk to a description of his son's behaviour and of his efforts to improve him. He had told us nothing of himself nor of the family relationships. Since such knowledge was indispensable to our insight into the problem, I turned the conversation in this direction. The family consisted of the father, the stepmother, a brother two years older who was about to enter the university, and a stepsister of five. The father had been married to the stepmother for twelve years and the five-year-old girl was a child of this marriage. The relationship between the parents, as well as the economic situation, was good. That the boy could have any feeling of inferiority in relation to the older brother seemed to the father out of the question, as the two had always been treated alike and had got along well together until this one began to behave so badly. Now they quarrelled all the time. The father thought that the stepsister was so much younger that there could be no question of jealousy of her. He did not pay much attention to her, was neither very affectionate with her nor unpleasant to her. The father was bitter, and complained that the change in the boy had completely disturbed what had formerly been a peaceful, happy family life. They used to sit around in the evening reading aloud, singing, or playing. Now when he got home at night he heard nothing except his son's misdemeanours, and he often had to go out on the street to look for him. The son had begun to learn the trade of shoemaker against his father's wishes. He had failed in the seventh grade and had refused to repeat the year. All arguments with him were in vain. He insisted on becoming a shoemaker like the stepmother's father. I inquired about the boy's relationship to girls, wondering if that could offer any explanation for his first running away. The father stated definitely that he knew his son's attitude toward girls and that this was impossible. When I asked how he explained this sudden change, he said, "Either the devil's got into him or he's gone crazy."

"Then he would not belong in our institution," I remarked.

The father answered, "Oh, you must not take that remark literally, but this has all happened so suddenly."

I talked to the boy alone. He was a very thin young man who looked somewhat older than his seventeen years. He was well dressed. The following is a part of the conversation, given verbatim.

"Do you know where you are?"

"No."

"In the child-guidance clinic of the Juvenile Court."

"Oh yes. My father wants to put me in a reform school."

"Your father has told me what has happened and I'd like to help you."

"It's no use." He shrugged his shoulders and turned away.

"Certainly it's no use, if you don't want help."

"You can't help me."

"I know you don't have much confidence in me; we don't know each other yet."

"Not that, but anyway it's no use." He showed the same hopeless, unco-operative air.

"Are you willing to talk to me?"

"Why not?"

"I must ask you various questions and I'll make you a proposition."

"What?" The tone betrayed expectation.

"That you don't answer any question you don't like."

"How do you mean?" He was astonished and incredulous.

"The questions you don't like you need not answer or you may tell me it's none of my business."

"Why do you say that?"

"Because I'm not a detective nor a policeman and I don't need to know everything. Anyway you wouldn't tell me the truth if I asked questions you didn't like."

"How do you know that?"

"Because that is what everybody does and you are no

exception. I wouldn't tell everything either to someone whom I'd met for the first time."

"But if I talk and tell you lies, will you know that too?"

"No, but that would be too bad. And anyway it isn't necessary because I don't want to force you to answer me."

"At home they always said if I'd talk, nothing bad would happen to me, but when I did it was always much worse. So I quit talking."

"But here it's a little different. I'll be satisfied with what you are willing to tell. But I'd like to be sure you are telling me the truth."

"Good."

"You agree?" I offered him my hand which he took eagerly.

"Agreed."

You will understand this type of introduction and its purpose better when we take up the question of the emotional contact between the worker and the patient. You will soon see what a good relationship I had established with him.

"What grade were you in when you left school?"

"Seventh."

"Why didn't you go further in school?"

"I failed in three subjects and didn't want to go any more."

"Did your father agree to that?"

"He would have liked it better if I had repeated the grade."

"How did you happen to take up shoemaking?"

"My grandfather is a shoemaker and I wanted to be one too."

"I'm not interested in knowing all about your troubles, but how did they begin? Why did you go to Graz?"

"I don't know."

"There must be some reason, though, why you went there. You might just as well have chosen another city."

"I really don't know."

"But it's not so long ago, not even a year. Think a little; maybe it will occur to you."

"Perhaps because my brother went there a year ago with a holiday group." Here he hesitated and became silent.

"Don't you want to tell me something more?" I asked this question after a pause during which I had noticed that the boy was having a battle with himself and was unable to come to a conclusion. He looked me straight in the eyes, then bowed his head, and shaken with sobs, said:

"If you promise you won't tell my father, I'll tell you something."

"Here's my hand on it." He took my hand and shook it vigorously.

"I wanted to kill myself."

"When?"

"Last summer."

"Before you got the money from your father or afterwards?"

"Before."

"Why?"

"My brother went away with mother to visit an aunt, and since I was an apprentice I had to stay at home. I went to work for a week. Then I laid off for three days and suddenly got afraid my father would find it out. Then I wanted to kill myself."

"Did you try to kill yourself?"

"No. I thought I'd go away and never come back. I got the money from my father and started off. When the money was all gone, I didn't know what to do and came back home. At home there was an awful row and since then everything's been all wrong."

"How do you get along with your brother?"

"All right; we used to get along better, but now he is on father's side."

"Do you think the other children are treated better at home than you?"

"No!"

"Doesn't it matter to you that your brother is getting educated and that you are a shoemaker's apprentice?" To this question he made no reply.

He went on to report the following facts. He was four when his mother died. His father remarried a year later. His stepmother was much attached to her father, the shoemaker, who according to the boy must have been a very understanding man. The tender attachment he had had to his own mother he transferred very quickly to the stepmother. The relationship to his father also had been good until the previous year. Despite his present antagonism to his father, he described him as a good man who stayed at home in the evenings, went seldom to beer taverns, and spent a great deal of time with his children. There was no great financial strain.

It is interesting to note how the boy justified the money episode. His father gave the brother money for the trip with his mother; therefore he had a right to the same amount. Had he told his father his true reason for wanting the money, of course it would have been refused. Consequently, he lied. It was not yet clear why he held his father responsible for his becoming a shoemaker. He said: "Father should have known better than I. I was dumb. A fourteen-year-old boy doesn't know what he wants to be. My father should have made me repeat the seventh grade. If he'd only insisted, then I would have obeyed and today I'd still be in school."

After a while I asked him if he thought it was possible for him and his father to come to some understanding. I offered to help. He was sceptical, but not so reluctant as at first. He said, "Oh, I've talked to my father time and again. It's no use." I tried to make him see that his father could not understand him as long as he did not know what he was really thinking. He might let me try to explain to the father. He released me from my promise to say nothing.

The boy went into the next room and sent his father to me. I had to talk with his father a long time before I could make him see that, without knowing it and without meaning to, he had lived with his son and had not been able to understand him. I told him also what the boy had suffered as a result of this situation. At first he listened in astonish-

ment and shook his head incredulously; then he became in-
dignant. Finally, as he began to understand, he was unable
to restrain his tears. He apologized and said that he had not
wept so since he was a child. I reassured him by saying that
it was a natural reaction to such a realization and that I
took it as proof of his affection for the boy. He calmed
himself and was in such a conciliatory mood that I thought
it was an opportune moment to begin to effect an understanding between father and son.

I must interpolate something here in order to avoid a
misunderstanding. I have told you that it is wrong in a
situation of conflict to induce a compromise by talking each
of the participants into conceding a little. What I attempted here with this boy and his father does not contradict my former statement. This talking things over accomplished the purpose in that it enabled the son to tell his
father what motivated his conduct and it thereby restored
his lost relationship to his father. This placed the formerly
good relationship upon a more secure basis.

So I called the boy back. I started the conversation along
these lines and then left them alone, feeling that a third
person would only prove a hindrance. After about twenty
minutes, I came back to find them both red-eyed and silent.
The father said in answer to my look of astonishment, "It's
no use, he won't talk." I know that the mentor dare not let
himself get angry and I know that I should have been able
to understand the father's emotional situation, but I was
angry and disappointed in him. I had worked with him
for over two hours to show him how the situation had arisen

and had tried to show him what he must do to bring the poor boy back into a sympathetic relation to him, and now he was behaving like this! Without looking at the father, I went over to the boy, put my hand on his head, and said, "Never mind, one doesn't always have to talk. Two people can understand each other without saying a word." At that the boy began to cry violently. I do not know just how it happened or who took the initiative, but the next minute they were in each other's arms. I must admit that I too was not untouched by the scene. After things were a little calmer, I wanted to get the boy out of the way in order to say something important to the father, so I sent him out to buy me some cigarettes. I made it as clear as I could to the father that such a first reconciliation was far from being the end of the conflict. He could expect that his son would prove even more troublesome in the near future. Since there was no time then for a longer interview, I advised him to come back to me as soon as his son misbehaved again in order to consult me before he undertook any disciplinary measures. At the boy's suggestion, we arranged that he and the father should go straight from me to his employer so that he could get back to work that afternoon. The boy seemed relieved and pleased. Father and son went away arm in arm as though a lasting harmony had been established.

Early the next morning I found the father in despair, waiting for me at the door of the clinic. He poured out a flood of complaints. "It's no use. We can't do a thing with that boy. He must go to the reform school. You saw how broken-up he was yesterday, and now it's the same old story again. Kindness doesn't work with him."

I asked calmly, "But what's the matter?" You will understand that I was not especially disturbed. I had told him the day before that something more was bound to happen. I was surprised, however, that it had happened so quickly. The father continued, "We went away entirely reconciled. On the way I gave him a good talking-to, to the effect that he must keep on being good now since I had forgiven him. He listened and said nothing, so that I had to keep myself in hand not to get angry again. I didn't give his employer any explanation because he thinks that the boy was sick. Instead of beginning work in the afternoon as he should have, he went bumming around until late that night."

You will remember that I had sent the boy out for cigarettes in order to call the father's attention to the fact that backsliding was to be expected. Now it had occurred. Although the father should have been prepared for this by my talk, he had lost control of himself, had reproached his son severely, and had jeopardized what we had achieved on the preceding day. It is understandable that the father's participation made the boy seem to play the role of the "ungrateful prodigal." Such critical situations are usually misunderstood by parents and often by educators. Since the real situation is seldom properly recognized, we find ourselves on the wrong track and endanger the success of all our pedagogical efforts.

What occurs in these dissocial young people has a great

deal to do with unconscious guilt feelings. We shall go into that later. However, we can now clarify some of the determining factors. It is comprehensible that a boy who has been accustomed to severe punishment for his misdemeanours should feel distrustful when the punishing person, the father, suddenly shows a right-about-face attitude. This change is not trusted and is therefore put to further tests; confidence is established only when the boy is convinced that the punishment is really abandoned. The dissocial youth is not satisfied when he gets kind and gentle treatment from his superiors; he aggravates them through increasingly annoying behaviour. Instead of understanding this, the parents may take this behaviour as proof that he cannot be influenced through kindness and consideration. They begin again with severity, and soon the old situation is restored, and no improvement can be expected. However, if the father shows real understanding and does not let himself make the mistake of falling back into the old attitude, then a critical situation arises for the youth. The antagonistic conduct, motivated by defiance of the father, has no longer any meaning. When the dissocial behaviour begins as an expression of distrust, it is as though the child said to the parents, "Treat me the way you used to." You will understand this better when we discuss the aggressive type in Chapter Eight.

It is only when the provocative behaviour fails to achieve its aim that this pattern which supports the delinquency breaks down. Then gradually the manifestations of delinquency recede. The period of time necessary for this is indefinite; it varies according to how deeply the motivation is anchored in the unconscious. We are dealing here with a process which I have often observed but for which no adequate theory has been worked out. Such a theory can be evolved only when a sufficient number of such cases has been analysed.

Let us go back to our case. I now saw that the father because of his emotional situation could not be counted on as a therapeutic helper and that I must work without him. I learned that the boy was at present at work and asked the father to send him to meet me that evening. I often have young people who work come to meet me on my way home in the evening. He met me punctually and was cordial though not communicative. He belonged to that group of people who talk little, but who are pleased to have someone with them. I asked him how he was and how he had got along with his work the past two days. He lied to me with a glib assurance about everything he had done the day before whereas I knew that he had not been in the workshop. We mentioned his father and he remarked that I really did not know his father. When I asked what he meant, he said, "You think he's a lot better than he really is." "Is he so bad then?" "No, but he is not good to me. He nagged me all the way home yesterday. He said I had to be good now that he'd forgiven me."

We have here an indication why the boy had reverted to his former behaviour so quickly. The father, who tried to talk him into something, seemed to him not to be the understanding person he had appeared in our interview. He had forced the boy back again into a bad position. As we talked, we walked slowly along the street. It began to rain and I thought I had better take a trolley. He was unwilling to leave me and came along. Among other things, we talked about music, whereupon he lost some of his reticence and told me that his family was musical; his father played the violin, his brother the piano, and he himself the flute. When we reached his transfer point where I urged him to leave, he remained, saying he would go the whole way home with me. Just before we got out, he asked me when and where we could meet again. I gave him an appointment for three days later, whereupon he said, "That's too far off. Can't it be sooner?" I said, "Yes, if you want to meet me tomorrow evening at seven on Blank Street." He went with me to my door and said, "Please give my regards to your wife." My wife had never been mentioned; he did not even know that I was married, but took it for granted. I stood by the door watching him as he walked away. After about fifty steps, he turned and raised his hat and I did likewise. This was repeated several times, until he reached the corner. The next evening he was there right on the dot. He proposed that we walk rather than ride so that we need not part so soon. Walking this distance took about an hour. Again he did not talk much but he invited me to come to his house some evening to hear some music. It was not certain that his father would play, but his brother had already promised to accompany him on the piano. I said that I was a very severe musical critic and that he and his brother must really get up a good programme before they could expect me to come. You will understand that I wanted to turn his own impulse to account pedagogically and I therefore utilized this interest, which would keep him occupied at home over a long period of time.

Since I was very busy during this period I could give him only a half hour three times a week and this had to be on my way home in the evening. If I were going to be able to achieve anything remedial with him under such unfavourable circumstances, he must develop some strong emotional feeling for me. It was not wise to question him directly. The only way I could appraise his feelings was to put them to the test, and so I told him to come to meet me two hours earlier than I knew I could be there. When I got there, he was gone. I learned that he had waited more than an hour and a half. He was not irritated when he left, but had left a request that I should let him know when and where we might meet again. We met the next day. I decided to praise him for his long wait as soon as a good opportunity presented itself. I did not have long to wait. He was friendly, did not reproach me, but on the contrary said he understood that I had a great deal to do and could not always keep appointments. Again we walked. He talked about his employer and told me jubilantly of some new work which had been entrusted to him. Through it all, I could see clearly a new feeling of his own importance. He talked also of the disagreeable things in the shop. Another worker was jealous of him and was cross and grouchy if he whistled a tune,

something he had of late especially enjoyed. Then he began
to talk about home. He became particularly expansive over
the musical programme. He was very pleased with his
brother, who was co-operating with him very well. This
showed me the direction in which I could reward him. I
thought it well to settle on a date, but since I wanted things
to become a little more stable at home I put it off until Sunday, two weeks following. He was very happy to know that I
would come on a certain day and was not impatient that
he had to wait so long. We walked along in silence; he was
lost in his thoughts and I was busy watching him. After
a while I asked him what he was thinking about. He was
embarrassed and did not want to tell me. When I pressed
him, he said that it was really too stupid, he was not thinking about anything in particular, perhaps I'd only laugh
at him if he told me but things were always like that with
him. At first something would seem very important to
him; he could not express it to his own satisfaction, he
could only intimate it. If the other person did not show any
interest, he would suddenly feel he had made too much fuss
about something unimportant and would be embarrassed
and unable to open his mouth. I made him understand that
I did not expect anything remarkable from him and if it
cost him too much effort he should remain silent. We went
a little further and then he began timidly, "If my father
were only like you, I would never have done all those things."
I took that as an opening for talking about his relationship
to his father. What he said was in substance only what we
already know. The next three interviews were concerned

mostly with various members of the family and in many points they clarified his relationship to his father.

One Saturday, after a week's separation, he turned up beaming. His pay had been raised a third. This was even more surprising since he had already received a slight increase in pay two weeks before. This, in addition to the fact that he had been entrusted with more important work, shows us that he had developed a new attitude toward his work. We see too that it can be materially advantageous to reach an inner equilibrium. The employer had certainly not raised his pay out of love for the boy nor out of interest in his re-education. As a matter of fact he was ignorant that any such remedial training was going on. I would like to make it clear here that, as a matter of principle, I do not make any contact with the employer or the place of work. However helpful that might prove at times, it is too dangerous to risk as it may only bring the youth into a more difficult position. Employers and fellow-workers could thus learn things which, in case of trouble, they could use against the youth.

Now to the Sunday visit! The family were all at home. The boy was greatly excited and I tried to put him at ease by asking them to begin. They played better than one would have expected. The boy was on fire with enthusiasm. I let him see plainly that I was pleased, but did not overdo my appreciation. The situation was natural; the whole family was happy, as I could read in their faces, and they were more than cordial to me. During a short pause, we sat around the table discussing various things, the mother's household affairs, the father's work, and the like, but nothing was said about his son's former or present behaviour. I stayed for nearly three hours.

The father, pleased with the outcome, came with me part of the way home. He was just as enthusiastic now as he had been despairing several weeks before. And just as then I had to curb his despair because all was not lost, so now I had to curb his enthusiasm because all was not yet won. Unpleasant surprises were not yet excluded. He said, "It seems like a dream to me that I could have been so discouraged that I wanted to put that boy in an institution. I didn't know what else to do. It's just like old times now. He works regularly and his employer told me he was completely satisfied with him. He comes home in the evening promptly, gets out his flute, and the two boys play together for hours. We're really a united family again. I can't tell you how happy I am that everything is all right once more."

The next evening I met the boy again. I did not have much time for him as I had an appointment. He went on the street car with me, talked over details of my visit, and closed with, "I went to bed right afterwards and I had to think it all over again, it was so nice." We continued meeting a few weeks longer, and though he walked all the way home with me, he did not come into my house because I wished to avoid that. Our meetings were interrupted by my vacation. During such a period, I do not give up the relationship already established but I keep in touch with the boy through letters. I exert myself to avoid everything that will weaken the transference at a time when it is pedagogically effective. A long separation without correspondence would constitute such a disturbing factor. That this relationship must be broken off later is obvious, but this question will be taken up in another chapter. He was an enthusiastic letter writer. He wrote at least once a week, and if I replied immediately, twice. In one of these letters he reported that his mother and sister had gone to visit relatives. The mother had wanted to hire a woman to help with the housework while she was gone but he had thought this unnecessary and had offered to keep house himself. He told me about the bachelor housekeeping and how his father and brother must take orders from him. If they did not behave, he made a scene, and his father gave in more quickly than his brother, with whom he often had to be severe. Gradually the letters became cooler in tone although they arrived as frequently as before. When I came home, I let him know and he came to our next appointment with his old enthusiasm. He asked how I was and seemed pleased when I told him that we could meet in our usual way two days later. He did not come but wrote me a note excusing himself and asking if we could postpone the meeting until two days later. I agreed but he failed to turn up again and sent no excuse. I was not annoyed by his not coming. However, I cannot say that I was pleased with his release from me because it seemed to have occurred too quickly. I became a little anxious about him and feared that he had fallen back into his old ways. I was far from thinking that a permanent result had been accomplished. I wrote to him and received an immediate reply. He said that things were going well and that at present he was working overtime in the evening and therefore could not meet me. In a few weeks the rush would be over and he would be glad to see me again. By chance I met his father and he spoke with approbation of the excellent behaviour of the boy and said he hoped it would continue.

For several weeks I did not see him. At Christmas he came to see me, sent me a card at New Year's, and then I did not hear from him for many weeks. In the spring I met him by chance in the street car. He was in the best of spirits. For the next year and a half I had letters from him now and then, especially at holiday times. As far as his retraining went, the task was finished. He continued to do well for three years. We must recognize, however, that this boy had many other adjustments to make, among them a satisfactory heterosexual relationship.

Without an analysis of this boy, we can never be sure of the real reasons for the delinquency; we can only point to possible or apparent causal factors. The surprising features in this case, which are certainly not convincing without analysis, are the quickness and permanence of the therapy. To the psychoanalyst, it is clear that this therapeutic result was accomplished through the transference. The question whether permanent results can in general be obtained in this way will be taken up later.

It seemed clear that we were dealing in this case with an act of revenge against the father. The boy felt inferior to the brother because as a student he had advantages which were denied an apprentice. Yet it is not entirely clear why at seventeen he reproached his father and made him responsible for the fact that he had become a shoemaker, when at fourteen he had put up such a stubborn resistance against his father's wish to keep him in school. We know from both the father and the son that the job of shoemaker's apprentice was not agreeable to the boy. At that time, the incentive to be a shoemaker's apprentice must have been stronger than the wish to continue in school. This incentive later disappeared. A sixteen-year-old boy is no longer in the same psychological situation as a fourteen-year-old. We must therefore try to reconstruct the psychological situation of the boy when he began his apprenticeship. One of his statements gives us a clue. As we stood at my door the first evening, he said, "Please give my regards to your wife." This is not just a chance remark nor one called forth by mere politeness as we had never spoken of my wife. Either he had noticed my wedding ring or he took it for granted that I was married. In any case, my marriage was a fact to this boy: else he would not have sent his greetings to my wife. This assumption is further understandable since he had put me in the place of his father. We recall how he said to me later, "If my father acted toward me the way you do, then I wouldn't have done these things." It is in this connexion that we can understand that the greetings to my wife were in reality for his mother. When such utterances come forth without any demonstrable external stimulus, they come out of the unconscious and must somehow involve a great deal of affect. Can we assume that there was such a strong tie to his mother? She had been dead for a long time and the stepmother had long been a member of the family circle. We might risk this possible conclusion because we can find some grounds for it. In the first place a feminine habitus, an anxious, shy behaviour, had already made us think of an infantile incestuous tie. The relationship to his stepmother was very good, as we learned first from his father, then from the boy, and finally from our own observation. His love for his own mother he seemed to have transferred completely to his stepmother. The infantile incestuous tie was still in operation, the wave of repression in adolescence was stronger than normal—that is to say, he had not succeeded in giving up his love object within the family in favour of one outside. We see the same attitude to women in this boy that we did in the other youth; he turns away from them. In such cases the father remains the unconscious rival for the mother's love. The antagonism is repressed because one must love one's father. When, because of this repressed and unconscious antagonism and rivalry, the boy refused to go to school, he achieved satisfaction for his unconscious desire for revenge against his father. He knew that this would upset his father, particularly since he was a chief clerk and wished his son to have a similar position. The boy was not satisfied, however, with being unwilling to study; he went further and became a shoemaker like the stepmother's father. We know that the stepmother was tenderly attached to her own father. If the boy became a shoemaker, then he would force his stepmother to value him more than she did *his* own father, even as much as she did *her* father. We now realize that the father's efforts to keep him at his studies would have proved in vain even if he had not failed in school.

Two years later, when the dissocial behaviour began, he was in a different psychological state. We can imagine that the affective motive which had led him to be a shoemaker had been weakened by the unpleasant experience of being an apprentice. This must have been hard for a child of middle-class family who undoubtedly felt himself socially degraded, especially since he went to the workshop directly out of school. Furthermore he was always comparing himself with his student brother. The brother's vacation in a camp had made a deep impression on him. His sacrifice for his stepmother, that be became a shoemaker, was also in vain; she took his brother, not him, to visit her relatives. It would be comprehensible if hate had sprung up in him against his stepmother and had found an outlet in aggression toward her. But we see nothing of this. We must remember in this connexion that between the time of leaving school and becoming an apprentice, and the time of running away when he was sixteen, two years had elapsed. During this period he had lived through an interval of puberty and was in another developmental phase. Although the power of repression was still strong, the surge of libido had markedly strengthened his masculine aggression. He had no conscious hate feelings against his mother which would have been the case had the incestuous tie to her not abated. The loosening of this tie makes an approach to his father possible. He had actually tried to return to his father. He induced his father to give him money, and rationalized this by the fact that his brother had been given travelling money also. This gave him the same relationship to the father that the brother had. That he chose an objectionable way to bring himself closer to his father does not alter the fact. He did not recognize that he had taken an unfortunate path; he realized only that he had failed. We can imagine the conscious and unconscious struggle that raged in the boy: the disagreeable experiences as an apprentice, the father's disapproval of his being a shoemaker, the effort to hold his father as love object although his father had repulsed him and was at the same time a rival for the love of the stepmother; the futility of the sacrifice for his stepmother, and finally the feeling that the way back to his father was barricaded against him. It is not surprising that the boy, who saw his whole life plan disturbed, should think about killing himself. That he only carried his suicidal intentions out symbolically in the running away was due to his self-love, in psychoanalytical terms, his narcissism. This enabled him after much hesitation to find a way out of his torment.

This case demonstrates what we can learn about the causes of dissocial behaviour without going deeply into the matter as in a psychoanalysis. The theoretical implications in the therapeutic process will be made clearer when we discuss the "transference" in the next chapter.

SIX

THE TRANSFERENCE

WE have used the term "transference" several times, and in the last case we attributed the therapeutic results to the transference without further definition of the word. We shall now consider more closely the emotional relationship which is thus designated. During a psychoanalytic treatment, the patient allows the analyst to play a predominating role in his emotional life. This is of great importance in the analytic process. After the treatment is over, this situation is changed. The patient builds up feelings of affection for and resistance to his analyst which, in their ebb and flow, so exceed the normal degree of feeling that the phenomenon has long attracted the theoretical interest of the analyst. Freud studied this phenomenon thoroughly, explained it, and gave it the name "transference." We shall understand later why he chose exactly this term.

I cannot reproduce for you all of Freud's research about the transference, but must limit myself to essentials. When we speak of the transference in connexion with social re-education, we mean the emotional response of the pupil toward the educator or counsellor or therapist, as the case may be, without meaning that it takes place in exactly the same way as in an analysis. The "counter-transference" is the emotional attitude of the teacher toward the pupil, the counsellor toward his charge, the therapist toward the patient. The feeling which the child develops for the mentor is conditioned by a much earlier relationship to someone else. We must take cognizance of this fact in order to understand these relationships. The tender relationships which go to make up the child's love life are no longer strange to us. Many of these have already been touched upon in the foregoing chapters. We have learned how the small boy takes the father and mother as love objects. We have followed the strivings which arise out of this relationship, the Œdipus situation; we have seen how this runs its course and terminates in an identification with the parents. We have also had opportunity to consider the relationships between brothers and sisters, how their original rivalry is transformed into affection through the pressure of their feeling for the parents. We know that the boy at puberty must give up his first love objects within the family and transfer his libido to individuals outside the family.

Our present purpose is to consider the effects of these first experiences from a certain angle. The child's attachment to the family, the continuance and the subsequent dissolution of these love relationships within the family, not only leave a deep effect on the child through the resulting identifications; they determine at the same time the actual form of his love relationships in the future. Freud compares these forms, without implying too great a rigidity, to copper plates for engraving. He has shown that in the emotional relationships of our later life we can do nothing but make an imprint from one or another of these patterns which we have established in early childhood.

Why Freud chose the term "transference" for the emotional relationship between patient and analyst is easy to understand. The feelings which arose long ago in another situation are transferred to the analyst. To the counsellor of the child, the knowledge of the transference mechanism is indispensable. In order to influence the dissocial behaviour, he must bring his charge into the transference situation. The study of the transference in the dissocial child shows regularly a love life that has been disturbed in early childhood by a lack of affection or an undue amount of affection. A satisfactory social adjustment depends on certain conditions, among them an adequate constitutional endowment and early love relationships which have been confined within certain limits. Society determines these limits just as definitely as the later love life of an individual is determined by the early form of his libidinal development. The child develops normally and assumes his proper place in society if he can cultivate in the nursery such relationships as can favourably be carried over into the school and from there into the ever-broadening world around him. His attitude toward his parents must be such that it can be carried over to the teacher, and that toward his brothers and sisters must be transferred to his schoolmates. Every new contact, according to the degree of authority or maturity which the person represents, repeats a previous relationship with very little deviation. People whose early adjustments follow such a normal course have no difficulties

in their emotional relationships with others; they are able
to form new ties, to deepen them, or to break them off without conflict when the situation demands it.

We can easily see why an attempt to change the present
order of society always meets with resistance and where the
radical reformer will have to use the greatest leverage. Our
attitude to society and its members has a certain standard
form. It gets its imprint from the structure of the family
and the emotional relationships set up within the family.
Therefore the parents, especially the father, assume over-
whelming responsibility for the social orientation of the
child. The persistent, ineradicable libidinal relationships
carried over from childhood are facts with which social re-
formers must reckon. If the family represents the best
preparation for the present social order, which seems to be
the case, then the introduction of a new order means that
the family must be uprooted and replaced by a different
personal world for the child. It is beyond our scope to attempt a solution of this question, which concerns those who
strive to build up a new order of society. We are remedial
educators and must recognize these sociological relationships. We can ally ourselves with whatever social system
we will, but we have the path of our present activity well
marked out for us, to bring dissocial youth into line with
present-day society.

If the child is harmed through too great disappointment
or too great indulgence in his early love life, he builds up
reaction patterns which are damaged, incomplete, or too
delicate to support the wear and tear of life. He is incapable

of forming libidinal object relationships which are considered normal by society. His unpreparedness for life, his inability to regulate his conscious and unconscious libidinal strivings and to confine his libidinal expectations within normal bounds, create an insecurity in relation to his fellow men and constitute one of the first and most important conditions for the development of delinquency. Following this point of view, we look for the primary causes of dissocial behaviour in early childhood, where the abnormal libidinal ties are established. The word "delinquency" is an expression used to describe a relationship to people and things which is at variance with what society approves in the individual.

It is not immediately clear from the particular form of the delinquency just what libidinal disturbance in childhood has given rise to the dissocial expression. Until we have a psychoanalytically constructed scheme for the diagnosis of delinquency, we may content ourselves by separating these forms into two groups: (1) border-line neurotic cases with dissocial symptoms, and (2) dissocial cases in which that part of the ego giving rise to the dissocial behaviour shows no trace of neurosis. In the first type, the individual finds himself in an inner conflict because of the nature of his love relationships; a part of his own personality forbids the indulgence of libidinal desires and strivings. The dissocial behaviour results from this conflict. In the second type, the individual finds himself in open conflict with his environment, because the outer world has frustrated his childish libidinal desires.

The differences in the forms of dissocial behaviour are important for many reasons. At present, they are significant to us because of the various ways in which the transference is established in these two types. We know that with a normal child the transference takes place of itself through the kindly efforts of the responsible adult. The teacher in his attitude repeats the situations long familiar to the child, and thereby evokes a parental relationship. He does not maintain this relationship at the same level, but continually deepens it as long as he is the parental substitute.

When a neurotic child with symptoms of delinquency comes into the institution, the tendency to transfer his attitude toward his parents to the persons in authority is immediately noticeable. The worker will adopt the same attitude toward the dissocial child as to the normal child, and bring him into a positive transference, if he acts toward him in such a way as to prevent a repetition with the worker of the situation with the parents which led to the conflict. In psychoanalysis, on the other hand, it is of greatest importance to let this situation repeat itself. In a sense, the worker becomes the father or the mother but still not wholly so; he represents their claims, but in the right moment he must let the dissocial child know that he has insight into his difficulties and that he will not interpret the behaviour in the same way as do the parents. He will respond to the child's feeling of a need for punishment, but he will not completely satisfy it.

He will conduct himself entirely differently in the case of the child who is in open conflict with society. In this instance

he must take the child's part, be in agreement with his behaviour, and in the severest cases even give the child to
understand that in his place he would behave just the same
way. The guilt feelings found so clearly in the neurotic
cases with dissocial behaviour are present in these cases
also. These feelings do not arise, however, from the dissocial
ego, but have another source.

Why does the educator conduct himself differently in
dealing with this second type? These children, too, he must
draw into a positive transference to him, but what is applicable and appropriate for a normal or a neurotic child
would here achieve the opposite result. Otherwise the worker
would bring onto himself all the hate and aggression which
the child bears toward society, thus leading the child into
a negative instead of a positive transference, and creating
a situation in which the child is not amenable to training.

What I have said about psychoanalytic theory is only
a bare outline. A much deeper study of the transference is
necessary to anyone interested in re-educational work from
the psychoanalytic point of view. The practical application
of this theory is not easy, since we deal mostly with mixed
types. The attitude of the counsellor cannot be as uniform as
I have pictured it for you. We do not have enough description of individual forms of dissocial behaviour to enable us
to offer detailed instructions about how to deal with them.
At present our psychoanalytic knowledge is such that a
correct procedure cannot be stated specifically for each
and every dissocial individual.

The necessity for bringing the child into a good relationship to his mentor is of prime importance. The worker cannot leave this to chance; he must deliberately achieve it and he must face the fact that no effective work is possible without it. It is important for him to grasp the psychic situation of the dissocial child in the very first contact he makes with him, because only thus can he know what attitude to adopt. There is a further difficulty in that the dissocial child takes pains to hide his real nature; he misrepresents himself and lies. This is to be taken for granted; it should not surprise or upset us. Dissocial children do not come to us of their own free will but are brought to us, very often with the threat, "You'll soon find out what's going to happen to you." Generally parents resort to our help only after every other means, including corporal punishment, has failed. To the child, we are only another form of punishment, an enemy against whom he must be on his guard, not a source of help to him. There is a great difference between this and the psychoanalytic situation, where the patient comes voluntarily for help. To the dissocial child, we are a menace because we represent society, with which he is in conflict. He must protect himself against this terrible danger and be careful what he says in order not to give himself away. It is hard to make some of these delinquent children talk; they remain unresponsive and stubborn. One thing they all have in common; they do not tell the truth. Some lie stupidly, pitiably; others, especially the older ones, show great skill and sophistication. The extremely submissive child, the "dandy," the very jovial, or the exaggeratedly sincere, are especially hard to reach.

This behaviour is so much to be expected that we are not surprised or disarmed by it. The inexperienced teacher or adviser is easily irritated, especially when the lies are transparent, but he must not let the child be aware of this. He must deal with the situation immediately without telling the child that he sees through his behaviour.

There is nothing remarkable in the behaviour of the dissocial; it differs only quantitatively from normal behaviour. We all hide our real selves and use a great deal of psychic energy to mislead our neighbours. We masquerade more or less, according to necessity. Most of us learn in the nursery the necessity of presenting ourselves in accordance with the environmental demands, and thus we consciously or unconsciously build up a shell around ourselves. Anyone who has had experience with young children must have noticed how they immediately begin to dissimulate when a grown-up comes into the room. Most children succeed in behaving in the manner which they think is expected of them. Thus they lessen the danger to themselves and at the same time they are casting the permanent moulds of their mannerisms and their behaviour. How many parents really bother themselves about the inner life of their children? Is this mask a necessity for life? I do not know, but it often seems that the person on whom childhood experiences have forced the cleverest mask is best able to cope with reality. It is not surprising that the dissocial individual masquerades to a greater extent, and more consciously, than the normal. He is only drawing logical deductions from his unfortunate experiences. Why should he be sincere with those people who represent disagreeable authority? This is an unfair demand!

We must look further into the differences between the situation of social retraining and the analytic situation. The analyst expects to meet in his patient unconscious resistances which prevent him from being honest or make him silent; but the treatment is in vain when the patient lies persistently. Those who work with dissocial children expect to be lied to. To send the child away because he lies is only giving in to him. We must wait and hope to penetrate the mask which covers the real psychic situation. In the institution it does not matter if this is not achieved immediately; it means merely that the establishment of the transference is postponed. In the clinic, however, we must work more quickly. Talking with the patient does not always suffice; we must introduce other remedial measures. Generally we see the delinquent child only a few times; we are forced to take some steps after the first few interviews, to formulate some tentative conception of the difficulty and to establish a positive transference as quickly as possible. This means we must get at least a peep behind the mask. If the child is not put in an institution, he remains in the old situation under the same influences which caused the trouble. In such cases we wish to establish the transference as quickly as possible, to intensify the child's positive feelings for us that are aroused while the child is with us, and to bring them rapidly to such a pitch that they can no longer be easily disturbed by the old influences. To carry on such work successfully presupposes a long experience.

Let us interrupt our theoretical consideration here and see how the worker tries to grasp the situation, to establish the transference and to lift the mask. How others work, I do not know; I can only try to show you what I usually do. A youth comes into the consulting room. At first glance he seems to be the bully type. If we take a stern tone with him, he rejects us immediately and we can never get a transference established. If we are cordial and friendly, he becomes distrustful and rejects us or he takes this for weakness on our part and reacts with increased roughness. If we approach a boy who is intellectually superior with a severe air, he feels himself immediately on sure ground and master of the situation because he meets that attitude often in life. He looks with suspicion on people who are nice to him and is more than ever on his guard. The timid ones, who come in frightened, are easily reduced to tears by a stern demeanour and fall into a state which may be confused with sulkiness. How shall we conduct ourselves in order to establish a good contact with the child? I usually begin with a friendly look or attitude, sometimes I say, "How do you do," or I may only shake hands in silence. I say that there is nothing here to be afraid of, that this is neither a police station nor a court. Sometimes I tell a joke by way of introduction. This gives me an opportunity to size up the situation. We sit down opposite each other. Just how I proceed toward the establishment of the transference in an individual case depends on the impression I have of the youth as he first enters the room.

I consider this first moment of our coming together of

the utmost importance. It is more than a "feeling out" of the situation; it must have the appearance of certainty and sureness and must be put through as quickly as possible because in most cases it forms the foundation for our later relationship. The adolescent does the same thing when he comes into contact with me. He wants to know right away what kind of person he is dealing with. Children usually try to orient themselves quickly, but for the most part they are not clever about it. The adolescent, however, often develops an amazing ability at this. We can observe a momentary gleam in the eye, a hardly perceptible movement of the lips, an involuntary gesture, a "watchful waiting" attitude, although he may be in a state of conflict. The older he is, the harder it is to know whether he will prove stubborn, or openly scornful and resistant. It is especially difficult when he assumes an air of sincerity or unctuous submissiveness. If I accept this as genuine, he immediately feels superior although he may sense that I have the upper hand.

After this sizing up of each other is over, a struggle begins for the mastery of the situation. This may be brief or it may be prolonged, and I must confess that I do not always come out victorious. You must not think of this struggle, however, as a mutual show of conscious strength. There are many unconscious factors in it; we feel rather than know what actually takes place. My attitude from the very beginning lets the boy feel that I have a power over him. He is justified when he senses this as a danger. He does not feel this as an entirely new situation; he has experienced it often before. I am thus no different from his mother, father, or teacher. If he is a border-line case of neurosis with dissocial features, or a mixed form where the dissocial features are predominant, I remain in the position of the parents but, as our association progresses, I act somewhat differently. If the child is in open conflict and expecting an attack, he is disappointed. I do not ask him what he has done, I do not press him to tell me what has happened, and, in contrast to the police or Juvenile Court, I do not try to pry out of him information which he is unwilling to give. In many cases where I feel the child wants to be questioned so that he can come into opposition to me, I say that he may hold back whatever information he wishes, that I understand that one does not want to tell everything to a person he has met for the first time. When I add that I would do likewise, he is usually willing to fall into conversation with me about something remote from his difficulties but in line with his interests. To describe my attitude from the moment when I let the boy feel some activity in me, I would say that I become progressively passive the more he expects an attack from me. This astonishes him, he feels uncertain, he does not know where he stands. He feels, rather than understands, that I am not an authority with whom he must fight, but an understanding ally. I avoid the word "friend" intentionally since he has no friends; he allies himself with others only because he needs them to achieve some end.

In a natural fashion, I begin to speak of things which interest most boys but are in no way connected with their dissocial behaviour. Eight out of ten are interested in football. One must know the teams, the best players, the last match, the scores, etc. Less often one finds a contact through books, mostly through adventure and detective stories. It is often easy to talk about movies and in this way make the child lose his caution.

With little girls I talk about fairy tales and games. Often one does not need to go far afield. A remark about the clothes or jewellery they wear may start the ball rolling. I let the half-grown girls tell me about styles in clothes, in haircuts, or the price of toilet articles. I ask the youngest children who are afraid to talk what they like to eat; we discuss desserts and candies. Thus I reach topics which the child carries on in the conversation. Sometimes it is difficult, sometimes easy, but as a rule it is possible to arrive unobtrusively at what I wish to know. In the first interview I usually get the positive transference well enough under way to secure some explanations and to gain some influence.

It is also necessary to get some idea of the child's relationship to the members of the family and other people in the environment. Adolescent children usually answer such questions directly; with younger children this is more difficult. Either they do not answer questions at all or they answer in a way which is worthless for our purpose. We must learn their attitudes through various makeshifts, such as talking about games and stories.

I asked a ten-year-old girl if she liked to read. When she said "Yes," I asked what she liked best.

"Fairy tales."

"Without stopping to think, tell me the name of a fairy tale you like."

"Snow-White."

"What part in it?"

"Where the old witch sold Snow-White the poisoned apple."

"Were there pictures in your book?"

"Yes."

"One of the witch, too?"

"Yes."

"Describe the witch for me, not exactly as she is in the picture, but how you think of her."

She described the witch in detail, her size, her hair, her facial expression, mouth, teeth, and clothes. When I asked where she got these various characteristics, it turned out that they were a collection from people whom the child disliked. This does not always turn out so propitiously. Sometimes the figure described does not fit the disliked people in the environment.

Another little girl told me that she liked to play with dolls. I asked her to describe in detail a doll she would like to have. This again resulted in a composite figure, but this time it had the features of the people she loved.

A twelve-year-old girl once sat opposite me giving no sign through her facial expression, movement, or speech what kind of emotional situation she was in. I asked what colour she liked best.

"Red."

I continued, "When I think of a colour, I always think

of something which has that colour. On what do you see red?"

"On the front car of the grotto-train in the amusement park."

"Now tell me what colour you like least."

"Black."

"Where do you see black?"

"Your shoes and tie."

"But surely something else black occurs to you, too?"

"The hole where the grotto-train goes in is black, too."

What all this may symbolize need not concern us at the moment. We need only consider how the anxiety connected with the ride in the grotto-train has been displaced onto me. She sat in front of me in the same anxious tension that she sat in the train in the amusement park. Perhaps she wanted to ask, "What's coming next?" How do we know this? My shoes and my cravat (which was really grey) had for the child the same colour as the grotto which she did not like. You can see how we get material from which we draw conclusions about the psychological situation of the child. I certainly would not have received a satisfactory answer to a direct question, for even if she had been ready to tell the truth she would not have known how to describe how she felt.

In such a tense situation we can accomplish nothing. I let her tell me about the trip through the grotto. Brightly lighted pictures appeared suddenly in the dark, devils roasting poor souls on hellish fires, dwarfs digging in the bowels of the earth for treasure, and such things. Something uncanny was always appearing and nothing cheerful or happy ever happened. We went from this to the shooting galleries, from one stand to another, and to the merry-go-round. Then laughing, she told me about a funny fortune teller who could tell what was going to happen to you. When I asked what amusing experiences she could remember, she told of another trip to the amusement park at the time she was confirmed. With this her mood changed completely, making it possible for the transference to begin. She was now accessible to questions which came to the point. I do not need to mention the fact that the child had no conception of my intention.

Sometimes a deep distrust shows itself. Perhaps I have acted clumsily, perhaps I am dealing with a special type of personality. Then I must resort to some other method. I will report such a case where in a brief time I succeeded not only in overcoming the distrust but also in discovering how it arose.

A sixteen-year-old girl, who had been suspected of being a prostitute because of her behaviour and appearance, had suddenly shown a complete change. Her bold manner had disappeared and in her dress and behaviour she had become a conventional, respectable girl. The social worker wanted to know what had happened. Naturally I did not know, but asked to see the girl. We sat down together and she showed very evident distrust of me. I asked how things were at home but got no answer. Did she like to read? What did she think about? No answer. Would she tell me a dream? Continued silence. Thereupon I laughed and said, "You think it's dangerous to talk to me. I can understand that, but certainly it can't be dangerous to tell me the story of a movie you've seen." She laughed and started to tell about a circus acrobat who had to dive from a high place through a burning ring. Two girls were in love with him. One of the girls, out of jealousy, cut the wire and made him fall into the fire-ring. The second girl saved him but sacrificed her life to do so. As you can guess from this summary, the story did not tally exactly with what she had seen, but showed her own version of it. I asked her what pleased her best in it and got the answer I expected, namely, that the girl sacrificed herself for her lover. I then asked if she could remember how the hero looked. When she answered in the affirmative, I asked her to describe what he must look like to please her. She described him as a strong, young, slender, dark-haired, clean-shaven man with bright eyes. Now I said, "Tell me, what does Franz look like?" She understood immediately that I meant her boy friend, was a little embarrassed, and then described him to look just like the movie hero. She went on without further effort on my part to say that he was studying chemistry but her mother refused to let her go with him. It was clear that the change in the girl was to be ascribed to her affection for the man. By attacking her distrust, I soon succeeded in overcoming her resistance.

I shall now present a case to show you how the transference can help one to find the deeper-lying causes of dissocial behaviour.

A city school reported that for several months a thirteen-year-old boy had been absent on Tuesdays and Fridays. The history stated that instead of going to school he went to the horse market, not out of any special interest or because of the tips he may have got for small chores, but only to be in the neighbourhood of the horse-dealers. I do not regard every unusual bit of behaviour as springing from some obscure motive, but try first to find a simple explanation. Since I have always found that, after the transference is established, the child will go to school regularly if I show him that it pleases me, I tried it in this case. We must realize that in many cases no one troubles himself about a child's going to school and that he therefore has no incentive to endure the unpleasantness of school life. In such truancy cases, I have the boy come to me first every week, then every two weeks, and later less often. When he knows that I am interested in all the pleasant and unpleasant happenings in the previous school week, he enters into the school life, and the truancy subsides. With this boy who went to the horse market, the transference was established in the first interview. He came for the next two weeks and reported that he had been in school. The third week the mother came to say that he was going to school regularly, but twice a week he did not come home until late in the evening and she thought from the way he smelled that he must have been in the horse market again.

We see in this case how the transference blocked the outlet for a symptom. The force behind the symptom, however, was still effective and produced a new symptom. The boy could not stay away from school because of his feeling for me. Now we see that this was not a case of ordinary truancy. Something attracted him to the horses and it was only a coincidence that the time for school and the horses was the same. Through the transference, I could see that we were dealing with a deeper mechanism. One needs psychoanalytic methods in the treatment of such a case. I do not want you to conclude from what I have said that I have any hard and fast rules which enable me to establish the transference in all cases. I only want to protect you from making the crudest mistakes in your practice by giving you some hints from my own experience.

When the child comes to us in the institution, we do not feel obliged to hurry the establishment of the transference. Unless it is a case of neurosis with dissocial features, we are friendly, but show no extraordinary interest in him or his fate and do not force ourselves upon him. We ignore his distrust, his secret or open opposition, his condescension, scorn, or whatever he may show against us. The preparation for the transference he gets from his companions. He usually makes quick contacts with the other boys not because he shows his real self to them or because he needs friendship, but because he must have an audience to whom he can relate an exaggerated account of his adventures, for whom he even improvises new escapades when reality offers nothing impressive enough. According to his custom, he begins to collect information about the details of the organization and the people with whom he comes in contact. Is the counsellor a "good fellow," can he be annoyed or teased, and how? He hears a great deal from the boys who are

about ready to leave the institution. He learns the characteristics of the people on the staff, what the real life of the
institution is like. Through this contact with the other boys,
he saves himself from the disillusionment which often follows first impressions, and comes in touch with an authority
from which he does not need to turn distrustfully away, or
which he tolerates, with clenched teeth, until such time as
he attains his freedom and attempts a revenge.

If the *milieu* has done its part, the transference begins to
develop as the counsellor gradually lets himself be drawn
out of his passive role and responds to the newcomer in a
neutral but friendly manner. Sometimes he pays more attention to the boy, sometimes less. This fluctuation of interest is not a matter of indifference to the youth. If he is distrustful because the counsellor seems to pay undue attention
to him today, tomorrow he will be reassured if no notice is
taken of him. He betrays a definite excitement the next day,
however, if he thinks the counsellor has observed his un-
polished shoes with displeasure. The shoes will be more
highly polished or dirtier according to the positive or negative feeling aroused in him, or they will remain the same if
no transference is underway. In this case we must wait.
What I have said about the shoes is true for a host of other
small details which the educator must be quick to recognize
and to evaluate. He must sense the ambivalence or changes
from affection to distrust in the relationship of his charge
to him. There are no general directions for this. We must
observe at first-hand how the experienced counsellor directs
these waves of feeling and strives deliberately to raise the

crests to a higher point. It is easy to recognize when the positive relationship reaches a climax. Often the feelings of affection break out with such vehemence and strength that the child waits in great tension for his counsellor to appear, does something to attract his attention, runs after him, or finds something to do which brings him into his counsellor's vicinity. The unskilled worker will not recognize the importance of this moment, will be on the defensive and not realize that the affection of the boy can thus be changed into hate. On the contrary, when the hate reaction sets in, he will flatter himself that he has always seen through the hypocrite. If we try to show him how he misinterprets the situation, he turns a deaf ear. He does not understand that he is interpreting as cause what is really effect.

I would like to show you how hard it often is to establish a transference with individuals of the highly narcissistic type—that is, those who are in love with themselves. I cite the case of a seventeen-year-old boy who had gambled and speculated on the stock exchange and had made a lot of money. He had begun at fifteen as a cashier for a street money-changer, who entrusted him with orders on the exchange and made it possible for him to speculate on his own. He accumulated a small fortune for a boy, and made himself independent. He travelled to other countries and imported things which he sold as a bootlegger. This business paid well. He led a free and easy life in night clubs, gambled, and associated with the demi-monde. When his money gave out, he began pawning his mother's clothes. His mother, who had been left a widow after an unhappy marriage, had repeatedly tried to reform the boy. Since she could do nothing with him, she appealed for help to a social agency which brought him to us.

He was one of those boys who give no apparent trouble in an institution. Such youths are polite and obliging, handy and useful in simple office work. They know how to get along with others and soon achieve the role of gang leader. When one works more intensively with them, one learns to see their difficulties. Inwardly demoralized but outwardly as smooth as glass, they offer no point of attack. Their behaviour is a mask, but a very good one. They show no interest in the personnel, and ward off every attempt to establish a real relationship to them. Thus the transference, which must of necessity be very strongly positive if one is to accomplish anything with them educationally, is almost impossible to establish. In the institution they give the impression of being cured very speedily but when at large again they revert to their old behaviour. We must use the greatest caution with them.

Our man of the world knew how to withdraw from every effort to influence him. He was with us several months without any transference having been established in the psychoanalytic sense. We could see, however, that he had been influenced by the environment. I thought it a good idea to get him away from it for a time so that he could compare the discomforts of another environment with those which he enjoyed with us, feeling that this realization might make him accessible to therapy. For this purpose, however, he must not be sent away; he must go of his own accord. I had to avoid letting him know of my intention. The best way to achieve my purpose was to influence his feeling about the institution. Occasionally, running away from the institution takes place as the result of a sudden emotional state or because of a dream, and then it is hard to prevent. In most cases, however, it requires long preparation and should not escape the sharp eye of the counsellor. Aside from our position against punishment in general in a reform school, we regard it as a complete lack of understanding to punish returned runaways. The running away takes place only when the "outside" is a more attractive place than the "inside." If we can induce the boy to talk to us while he is in this conflict, we can often make the "inside" seem more attractive without mentioning his intention of running away. We can accomplish the opposite effect if we recall the outer world to his memory as more attractive than the life in the institution.

A short talk was sufficient to put our gambler in the right mood. A half hour after he left me, I got the report that he had run away. The first part of my treatment had worked. The counsellor did not know that I had provoked this. I confide such things to the personnel only when I need their co-operation, since it is extremely difficult when one lives among the boys to conceal such things. If such a plan does not succeed, it gives rise to unending differences of opinion. With our young gambler, this successful provocation to run away was a prologue to the establishment of the transference. I expected his return on the second day.

When he had not turned up after a week, I feared that I had made a mistake.

At nine o'clock in the evening ten days later, someone knocked on my door. It was the runaway. He was so exhausted physically and under such psychological tension that I felt I could accomplish much more with him than I had planned. I did not reproach him for going away, as he evidently expected. I only looked at him seriously and said, "How long has it been since you had something to eat?" "Yesterday evening." I took him into the dining room of my apartment where my family was at supper and had a place set for him. This boy, who was usually the complete master of a situation, was so upset that he could not eat. Although I was quite aware of this, I said, "Why don't you eat?" "I can't. Couldn't I eat outside?" "Yes, go into the kitchen." His plate was refilled until he was satisfied. When he had finished eating, it was ten o'clock. I went out and said to him, "It's too late for you to go into your group tonight. You can sleep here." A bed was fixed for him in the hall. I patted him on the head and said good-night to him.

The next morning the transference was in effect. How strongly positive it was I learned from a mistake which I made later. Without realizing it I gave him grounds for jealousy, in that I let one of his comrades check up on his bookkeeping, in which he often made errors. The counsellor to whom he was entrusted succeeded, however, in making good the mistake in this especially difficult case. Soon after this he was allowed to bring the supplies from the city. He never let himself be led astray after that. He left the institution to become a salesman and for years has had a satisfactory record as a clerk in a business establishment.

The establishment of the transference seldom necessitates such an artifice. Generally the ordinary course of events is enough. I reported this case merely to show you how impossible it is to lay down general rules.

SEVEN

THE TRAINING SCHOOL

It is often necessary to take a youth out of his environment and to put him into an institution in order to treat his dissocial behaviour. We would not see all that psychoanalysis has to contribute to re-education if we studied only individual cases of delinquency and did not go into the reformatories where numbers of dissocial children are brought together. We know that psychoanalysis offers great therapeutic possibilities in the treatment of individual cases. How can it help us in the institution? We shall find that here also the psychoanalytically trained worker is better equipped for his task than the worker without this training.

How can we apply psychoanalytic theory in the organization of a training school? In most institutions, the children live in groups in charge of a counsellor. This matter of grouping is of first importance. In the older type of institution the groups are for the most part composed of children with varying pathological conditions; this can serve only to aggravate the condition of the individual child. It is self-evident that we cannot do educational work with such a group; we can maintain control only through use of force. This may be one of the reasons why, in correctional institutions, it seems difficult to forgo corporal punishment.

In more modern institutions, two efforts are being made: (1) to separate the children into the smallest possible groups, and (2) to compose these groups in such a way that the group life will favourably influence the behaviour difficulties. For practical reasons it is impossible to assign a worker to each individual, nor should this be the aim of the organization. Re-education in an institution is and must remain a group training, which should be adapted to meet the special needs of delinquents. It is easy to understand why those who actually work with youth prefer small groups whereas the administration wishes to operate with large groups for reasons of economy. With the severest cases, even the administration will realize the advantages of a small group. I do not mean to say that grouping is considered an important matter in all institutions. There are many old institutions that have changed their names but are dominated exclusively by an economic policy. It is out of the question to expect any psychoanalytic understanding in these institutions.

The children in our institution were separated originally according to sex, and whether or not they had finished school. Otherwise they were left in groups which they had happened to join on arrival. Very soon, however, the management of these groups became so difficult that something had to be done. Since corporal punishment was ruled out from the beginning, we moved difficult individual cases about until we found a group where they could adjust themselves. The first grouping therefore arose out of these practical difficulties. There was one exception. One group consisted of those cases excluded from all other groups. Our experience and the intuitive judgment of some of our workers soon enabled us to place the children in a suitable group shortly after their admission.

By means of this grouping we brought fairly similar children together. The frequent recurrence of typical peculiarities within the group impressed the counsellor, who thus became aware of them and was enabled to devise methods suitable to these children. He could apply the same methods more effectively in such a group because it was homogeneous. Thus the children in the group found the most favourable conditions for their development and treatment, and the groups were therapeutically as well as economically advantageous.

What I have related of this grouping system is not for the sake of giving you a ready-made sample, but of showing you how the form was evolved in response to our practical needs. No psychoanalytic theory was involved in this plan. As I have pointed out, we followed an economic principle. Grouping is most effective when the mere living together has a favourable influence on the dissocial behaviour. The question then becomes: "Which types of dissocial behaviour are most favourably influenced by living together in such a group?"

From the psychoanalytic point of view, the manifest character of the delinquency is not important, but rather the psychic mechanisms which motivate the dissocial behaviour. We must find out in each case what these motives are before we can group the pupils in such a way that they will have a favourable influence on each other and thus be made fit to return to society. Psychoanalysis will help us more in the problem of grouping when it has uncovered these underlying mechanisms in a great number of cases of delinquency. However, we must not confuse this application of psychoanalytic knowledge with the actual psychoanalytic treatment of a delinquent. We refer here only to ways in which psychoanalytical application can help us in diagnosis.

The problem of grouping is not solved merely by bringing children together in the expectation that the interaction of their psychic mechanisms will operate therapeutically. Conditions other than those of the personality of the individual pupils must be considered. I refer to those external conditions which in general constitute the *milieu*. Not only are the companions with whom he lives important to the dissocial child, but also the material world around him; not only the *milieu* of the group but also the institution as a whole.

Let us consider the conditions in the old type of reformatory and in the new training school. In the former, we are struck by the surly, shut-in reaction of the inmates. Everywhere we meet a cautious, distrustful, antagonistic attitude. No one looks us straight in the eye. The usual happy overflowing of youthful good spirits is entirely absent. What cheerfulness there is to be seen strikes us as sad. Real joy in living expresses itself quite differently. We can hardly restrain a shudder at the dammed-up hate we feel in these young people. This antagonism finds no solution in the institution but is condensed and stored up for later discharge against society.

The superintendent of such an institution once called my attention to wash basins that had been in use for twenty years. He was proud of the fact that they had remained so long undamaged and still shone like new. In the dormitories the beds stood in a row, twenty-five on each side, like rows of soldiers, not an inch out of line. The covers were all folded at correct right angles and fell like a plumb-line. Everywhere was the same meticulous order. When we consider how hard it is to make most children orderly at all, we know what constant discipline is necessary to maintain such military order as this. If it is difficult for normal children to be neat, how much harder is it for dissocial children! They could not conform to the demands of society outside. Can we expect to socialize them through such methods?

Now for the other type of institution. If you had come to our training school on a particularly good day you would have found something like the following: Before you reached the grounds of the institution you might have met a local inhabitant complaining loudly that the delinquents, instead of being locked up and marched out in a line to go walking, were allowed to run around in the neighbourhood, that they could come and go at will through unlocked doors and gates. He is on his way to complain to the superintendent because some boys, who were scuffling on their way home, had broken one of his windows. You cannot see me at once because a policeman is waiting for me. From my office you hear the excited voice of a gardener complaining that he cannot have the boys coming into his orchard. I invite you to come in with the policeman and let you hear the account of what happened the day before. Two boys made a fire in the woods and cooked a trout that was obviously caught in a near-by brook, a thing forbidden by law. The policeman is no more than out of the room and we are on the point of making a round of the institution when the cook bursts in in great excitement to say that she had made just the right number of dumplings and five have disappeared. Maybe you will decide to forgo further inspection of the institution.

Is it better to have such a state of affairs in a training school or should one really depend on lock and key? In the consultation room of the clinic the worker accepts the misconduct of the delinquent and in the beginning does not interfere with it but awaits the time when a change comes of itself. We can see no reason why the procedure should be different in the institution just because there are more cases and the difficulties are greater.

It is characteristic of the delinquent that he possesses little capacity for repressing instinctual impulses and for directing energy away from primitive goals. He is thus unable to achieve what is considered by society a normal ethical code. The great majority of children in need of retraining come into conflict with society because of an unsatisfied need for tenderness and love in their childhood. We therefore find in them a proportionately increased thirst for pleasure and for primitive forms of instinctual gratification. They lack inhibitions and they have a strong, though distorted, craving for affection. If the delinquency is to be cured rather than repressed, we must meet these needs even though at first this seems futile to so-called "understanding people."

As a matter of fact, the work in our institution was misunderstood. Anxious, timid people were horrified, the neighbours were angry, and every time anything went wrong there was a great outcry. However, we did not let ourselves be misled. We utilized the daily conflict to achieve an educational purpose. We assured these youths of our interest and affection in an environment calculated to please them, made use of the love thus won from them to retrieve a neglected part of their development, i. e., the transition from their earlier unreal world of self-indulgence to one of reality.

From the very beginning we felt intuitively that above all we must see that the boys and girls from fourteen to eighteen had a good time. We did not treat them as dissocial or criminal individuals from whom society needed protection; they were human beings who had found life too hard, whose antagonism to society was justified, and for whom an environment must be created in which they could feel comfortable. With this attitude as an impetus, the work carried itself along. The faces of the children and the personnel reflected happiness. I can still remember the tension with which we awaited the first admission and how delighted he was when we threw ourselves into the task of winning him over. Later, we modified our treatment in many ways, but I can assure you that even our first exaggerated efforts did no harm. That first boy is well adjusted and has been successfully earning his living for years.

Without really knowing what we were doing we worked out what might be called a practical psychology of reconciliation, which can be used to advantage with most of the children in training institutions of the present time. It is of interest that the same types of delinquency which stirred us to friendliness and kindness provoke the personnel in the older type of institution to an attitude of stern moralism and revenge. I have never felt the need of changing my attitude in this respect but have continued to find it justified. To be sure, there are some delinquents who cannot be influenced by the method outlined above. We shall discuss them later.

Specific educational methods are far less important than an attitude which brings the child into contact with reality. We must give the pupils experiences which fit them for life outside and not for the artificial life of an institution. The more the life of the institution conforms to an actual social community, the more certain is the social rehabilitation of the child. There is a great danger in an institution that the individuality of the child does not develop along lines best suited to his needs but that rules are laid down in accordance with administrative requirements which reduce the child to a mere inmate with a number.

Let us recall our own childhood. What did it mean to us to have a drawer, a cupboard, a box, or a place that

belonged exclusively to us where we could hide our secrets
from our parents and brothers and sisters, which we could
put in order if it pleased us but could leave in disorder to
our heart's content? How is it in an institution? Everywhere enforced uniformity. Not a single spot reserved for
an individual! The walls of the institution cut the child off
from real life, force him into fantasy experiences so that
it becomes difficult for him to correct his wishful thinking
with reality. How different it is if the delinquent lives in a
colony in which he is allowed to feel the consequences of
every small event and yet to preserve his individual freedom!

You must not think that all of the delinquents in our institution were enchanted with the environment as soon as
they entered. Many remained for a long time astonished,
distrustful, and incredulous. The roughest, who heretofore
had submitted only to force, looked on us as weaklings who
dared not risk interfering with them. The intelligent looked
down on us as stupid people who let ourselves be taken in.
Thus everything was represented from overt opposition to
silent scorn. Knowing this, we made no attempt to win over
the newcomers with words. We let the environment take effect and waited for an opportune moment. Only after they
had settled down into the routine did we devise any individual methods.

The food problem in an institution should not be overlooked. Ethical values have no weight with the delinquent
at the beginning but he can be caught by his desire for food.
He wants an abundantly supplied table; he lays little im-

portance on the change in menu. He is seldom interested in quality, but quantity is of prime importance. He can never believe that his counsellor is in sympathy with him and on his side, if he gets cornmeal mush while the counsellor gets roast beef. In our institution there was only one menu, cooked on the same stove and in the same utensils. This must be a basic principle. The displeasure over the difference in what counsellor and pupil get to eat creates a great distrust, which is carried over to the whole relationship.

The atmosphere that prevails in the training school must proceed from the personnel. The optimistic attitude of the counsellor toward life, the cheerfulness with which he works, create an atmosphere in which remedial work can be carried on without great effort. Thus the counsellors are able to approach their pupils in such a way that the latter have confidence in them and feel their understanding. Most of these young people have never had their infantile need for affection satisfied. They have never experienced the happiness of a close relationship to the mother. They need love. This constitutes a great demand on the personality of the counsellor. He must be highly intuitive in order to know the right approach to the child. The science of education has nothing to offer him in this respect. It is not enough to comprehend what the child says and does; the worker must be able to "live" himself into the situation so that these experiences become his own.

A word to women workers in this field. Experience in our institution showed that schoolboys before adolescence should not be entirely under masculine influence. This is in agreement with what psychoanalysis has taught us concerning libidinal processes. It is much better when men and women are working together in the group. With the older boys this feminine influence is no longer necessary. It is wise, however, to have a woman oversee such matters as nursing and washing and to supervise order and cleanliness in the recreation rooms as well as in the dormitories. Such a person should not limit herself to housekeeping tasks, but should be ready when occasion arises to exercise her influence in the boys' training.

The cure of delinquency is fundamentally a problem of libido; that is to say, the most important thing is the child's feeling for the counsellor or, more generally, for the people of his environment. This we must recognize in institutional care. I have already explained how we try to direct the children's feelings toward us, to stabilize these feelings, and to make use of them. In spite of all our efforts, however, our institution was not a paradise and we often had conflicts and ugly moods. It was especially noticeable in those groups directed by women that a bad mood in the leader would communicate itself to the children, who in turn reacted unfavourably, until the situation became intensified to the point of open conflict. At that time I had no understanding of the cathartic effect of talking things over, but I did notice how the mood of the whole group changed with the mood of the teacher. Through repeated conferences and talks with individual workers, in which we often touched on personal matters, I succeeded gradually in building up a friendly and confidential relationship with my co-workers.

This in turn reacted on our charges so that finally the same feeling-tone dominated the whole establishment. We sacrificed none of our authority but we had taken away the children's fear of us and replaced it with their confidence.

The mechanism of the transference as explained by psychoanalysis showed me later how we had accomplished our results. It showed me also why it is so easy to talk about training children, whereas we learn what to do only from experience. What succeeds with one teacher can be a total failure with another. I consider that successful work in an institution without a strong bond of feeling between the superintendent and personnel is impossible. I cannot conceive that a dissocial youth can be re-educated without a strong, positive feeling for the people in his environment. The attitude of the worker toward the leader determines of itself the relationship between the worker and the child.

At this point, it seems important to warn you against a too hasty application of what we have learned. The temptation is great to apply conclusions which are suitable for dissocial children to the education of normal children. Although deep and far-reaching relationships exist between the training of the two groups, we are not ready to say with assurance where they coincide. Among our charges we find border-line cases and transitional states approaching neurosis and psychosis. Here our work touches the field of psychiatry. We also find border-line cases of delinquent children that approach the normal. In such cases, we concern ourselves with the family, with educational work done by child-welfare groups, and with movements for young people. Our main work, however, must always develop along separate lines.

We found that the cases in our institution came almost without exception from families where the home situation was disturbed, broken up, or disharmonious, regardless of the deeper underlying causes of their delinquency. It seems as if the shocks which the individual receives from society are endurable only when he finds a haven, which in our society the family normally offers. Given such a haven, the expressions of his instincts are held within bounds acceptable to society. When this is lacking, the equilibrium of these unstable individuals is all the more easily thrown out of balance.

These disturbances of equilibrium bring about lasting effects which must be treated by social re-education when they take the form of dissocial behaviour. The methods used in influencing these dissocial children, especially at first, must differ essentially from the education of normal children.

Let us return to the institution. We know that the character and intensity of the child's libidinal ties to the objects of his earliest environment determine the course of his later life. This agrees with our belief that our success in the treatment of delinquency is to be attributed to the fact that we influenced the later development of the libido in the direction of sublimation and compensation. I shall illustrate with two cases in our institution, one a sixteen-year-old boy who was considered schizophrenic by our psychiatric consultant, the other a seventeen-year-old homosexual.

The sixteen-year-old, who came from a very good middle-class family, was sent to us because of repeated stealing at home. He had been in several other institutions but showed no improvement. How serious the situation was can be seen from what the father said to me when he brought the boy to us: "He would have ruined us if we had kept him at home any longer." In our institution he was extremely irritable and difficult to handle; he imagined that the other boys did not like him and that they threatened him physically, and he was very aggressive against his companions, his counsellor, and others with whom he came in contact. He revenged himself on the superintendent, who he thought had insulted him, by defecating one night outside the latter's door. His delusion of grandeur expressed itself in the idea of becoming a leader of gangsters. He said he had built up a gang in the city of which he was the ruler, but his father reported that this was not true. His behaviour and speech bore out the diagnosis mentioned above.

The boy was physically strong but did not have normal intelligence. To find the right occupation for him, it was necessary to take advantage of his anal aggressive characteristics by providing work in which he could excel physically without exposing his limited intelligence. We had only the vegetable garden to offer him where he could work with fertilizer and dig in the earth. This turned out to be an excellent choice.

The seventeen-year-old was put to work in the tailor shop because we assumed that the making of men's clothes could serve as a sublimation for his homosexual strivings. We do not mean to imply, however, that every dissocial youth who is homosexually inclined must learn to be a tailor in order to become a useful member of society. Something about this boy made me try this. In five months he learned what usually requires three years. The master tailor called him a genius at tailoring. During this whole period, he tried only once to engage another boy in homosexual practices. Because of the breaking up of the institution, he was turned back into the community earlier than we had intended. However, he got employment in a big tailoring establishment and continued to do well.

Our successful choice of work in both these cases we owe to psychoanalytic insight. In psychoanalytic terms, it was economically advantageous to these boys to work eight hours a day at a task which automatically satisfied their psychological needs. Since we could not alter the sources from which the homosexual derives the energy for his psychic life, it became our task to direct this energy into socially acceptable channels. It seemed obvious that his perverse libido should find an outlet in useful work in the tailor shop rather than bring him into conflict with the police. I should add that the boy was sent to the tailor shop against his will and that for some months he was discontented. When the institution was broken up and he was on the point of leaving, I talked to him about what he had accomplished in the workshop. He said, "It's a good thing people aren't always allowed to do what they think they want to."

In both cases, our psychoanalytic understanding enabled

us to turn the dissocial libido into normally acceptable
channels of work and in this way to relieve the delinquency.
A thoroughgoing psychoanalysis would probably have
achieved more certain results. From a practical point of
view an analysis is impossible for every delinquent. It is
imperative, however, for those neurotic dissocial cases who
are so incorrigible that the group itself excludes them.

Although the choice of occupation for a boy in an institution is of greatest importance and although the choice is
made with respect to our psychoanalytic orientation, this
does not suffice to cure the delinquency. Finding the proper
work is only one of the means employed. Frequently we are
successful in alleviating the situation by an energetic intervention in the acute conflict or by diverting this conflict
into new channels. Such an example was our young man of
the world,[1] in which case my first task was to establish the
transference. You have seen in this case how his return in a
hungry, exhausted condition enabled me to accomplish
more than I had expected.

In a case of stealing within the institution I did not rely
on my intuition but deliberately created the situation I
needed. This case will illustrate again how the worker must
free himself from all stereotyped methods.

About this time, I read Dr. Rank's book, *Das Inzest-
motiv in Dichtung und Sage* (The Incest Motive in Poetry
and Saga), in which he introduces the Aristotelean theory
of catharsis. It occurred to me that we might use the conflict situation of our charges to introduce catharsis; that is,

---

[1] See page 138.

we could make the boy the hero of the drama. The first opportunity for trying this seemed to be a conflict over stealing.

We had an eighteen-year-old boy who had been expelled from a military school for stealing from his comrades and who had stolen at home and elsewhere. After he had been with us for several months, I put him in charge of the tobacco shop. The employees each contributed a certain amount to buy their tobacco in common. I told the cashier to keep an eye on the boy without letting him know and to report to me when any money was missing. Four weeks later, he reported that about half the sum taken in weekly was missing. This seemed to be the right moment to expose the boy to an emotional shock in order to bring about catharsis, although I had no clear idea how I was going to do this. Since I wanted to gain a little time I told the cashier to send the boy to me in the afternoon without telling him that anything was wrong. The boy came while I was still undecided what to do. I wished to keep him with me for a while, so I proposed that he help me dust my books and put them in order. What should I do? I must proceed in such a way that the situation would develop around the boy himself, so that his anxiety once aroused would become so intense as to be unbearable. The instant he realized that the catastrophe of exposure was unavoidable, his anxiety must be turned into an emotional outburst. This sudden change of affect would make him accessible to treatment.

The "drama" was played as follows. We began our work. I inquired how he was getting along and gradually we approached the topic of the tobacco shop. "How much do you take in each week?" He mentioned a certain sum. We continued to dust the books. After a pause, "Does the money always come out right?" A hesitating "Yes" of which I took no further notice. After another pause, "When do you have the most trade?" "In the morning." Then still later, "I must look in on you some time and go over your cash drawer." The boy was getting more restless all the time, but I ignored it, went on working and kept coming back to the tobacco shop. When I felt that I had intensified his uneasiness sufficiently I suddenly brought the crisis to a head. "Well, when we get through here I'll go and take a look at your cash." We had been working together for about an hour and a quarter. He stood with his back to me, took a book from the shelf, and suddenly let it fall. Then I took cognizance of his excitement. "What's the matter?" "Nothing." "*What's wrong with your cash?*" His face became distorted with anxiety, and he stammered out the sum. Without saying a word I gave him this amount. He looked at me with an indescribable expression on his face and was about to speak. I would not let him talk because I felt that my action must have time to take effect and so I sent him away with a friendly gesture. About ten minutes later, he came back and laid the money on the table, saying "Let them lock me up. I don't deserve your help— I'll only steal again." He was greatly excited and was sobbing bitterly. I let him sit down and I began to talk to him. I did not preach, but listened sympathetically to what he poured out, his thievery, his attitude toward his family and to life in general, and everything that troubled him. The emotion gradually receded, relieved by the weeping and talking. Finally I gave the money back to him, saying that I did not believe he would steal again; that he was worth that much to me. I said, too, that it was not a present, that he could smoke less and pay it back gradually. So that no one should know about this, however, he had better put the money back in the cash drawer. I told the cashier that the amount had been returned and that he need take no notice of the affair. In the course of the next two months, the money was actually returned.

It is not improbable that the contrast in emotion from fear to relief brought about the solution. Practically the treatment was effective; in the short time he stayed with us, he conducted himself well. Later he was employed as a draughtsman in a furniture factory and acquitted himself creditably. In this case, we had succeeded in arousing a strong emotion in him and in making use of it in his retraining. We must wait for further experience with this method to see in which cases it is applicable as a special technique.

We must take it for granted that some young people will steal in an institution. Some people will regard it as regrettable that stealing takes place in an institution and others will think it absurd to make use of stealing in a boy's retraining as in the above case.

After such a solution of a conflict, a very intensive transference sets in that is important for the further course of the retraining but that endangers the results if the worker does not see to it that this emotional relationship is later dissolved. It is easy to see how such an intense tie to the worker can be the cause of jealousy and how this, in turn, can motivate further dissocial behaviour. The transference is the most important aid in our work but it can have undesirable consequences if we do not understand the mechanisms involved.

The remedial treatment of the individual can begin only when the transference is established, whether this be in the consultation room or in the institution. Re-education, however, is not achieved through words, admonition, scolding, or punishment, but through what the child actually experiences. Through the *milieu* we created in our institution and through our type of leadership, we had opportunities every day to give the children experiences the deep effect of which helped to relieve their dissocial behaviour. Often we made use of the mood of the moment or created a situation to produce the desired mood. Sometimes we used bandit adventure stories, which the dissocial love, to secure a foothold for further educational work. I can give you no general directions how to proceed. Every educator must work out the details of his own technique. If he possesses the capacity for this work, he can learn through observation, experience, and earnest study of the problems. It is certainly true that you cannot make an educator out of every personality. A great deal of harm can be done by the dilettante in this work as well as by the professional worker who is not endowed for this task.

Perhaps our attitude to the children in the institution

may appear as something to be taken for granted. I should like to add that such an attitude makes tremendous demands on the workers. We must not forget the wide gap between knowing what should be done and being able to do it.

People have often inquired what special educational methods we used. We really had no prescribed methods. When anything happened, such as a fight, a theft, or any great disturbance, all inevitable in an institution, I sent for the participants to talk things over. This talking together and an attitude of forgiveness toward even the worst offences seemed to us our most valuable method. This served us well because we had the confidence of the children.

Our charges came to us with the difficulties which they could not settle for themselves, complaints, uncertainties, hopes and struggles, questions about things they did not understand, and sometimes with ideas and fantasies which were hard for them to disclose. Many came with hate and scorn of religion; some with deep religious feeling. We had often to clear up their doubts and misunderstandings, but always with great care not to force our own convictions on them.

Sometimes they came in embarrassment to talk about their first infatuations, or their love experiences, both imaginary and real. They represented themselves as Don Juan and Sir Galahad; they came with their sexual difficulties, their suffering, and their burdens. Only in special cases did we lead the talk to sex topics. Perhaps it would interest you to know that in our toilets there were none of the drawings and writings usually found in such places. These talks resulted in a better understanding of the child's make-up. However varied their behaviour was, it always gave us some hint of what was going on inside our charges.

It is easy to recognize the great variation in the attitude of the individual child toward his environment. We can differentiate two kinds of hate reaction. One type hates the environment quite openly, without any attempt at concealment. This hate varies in quantity from a mere intimation to open repudiation and deadly hate. When we group all these reactions together we see their similarity.

The second hate type appears less often. It is concealed and is harder to recognize. This group is obliging to the point of insistence, friendly to a degree of unpleasant intimacy, self-conscious to the point of arrogance. They are liars and intriguers; they tyrannize over their comrades in secret. All that they do and say becomes understandable when we recognize their hatred.

I have always found that this hate is a reaction to an unsatisfied need for love. In many cases it is objectively justified; in others it arises only from the child's subjective feeling. In the first type, the hate is the result of too little love, a repudiation by the parents. In the second, the hate comes from another source; the parents, disappointed in each other, expend too much libido on the child. The child feels that this love is not given to him for his own sake and reacts to it by becoming dissocial. Each group expresses its hate in a characteristic way: open insubordination to the point of brutality in one group; underhanded intrigue to cowardly murder in the other.

I must mention the "abnormal" cases in the institution before closing this chapter. By this I do not mean pathological cases, but only those bordering on neurosis or psychosis, young people with abnormal manifestations of affect which, however, have not developed so far as to lead them to a neurologist or psychiatrist. They are the most difficult cases for remedial training and I cannot go into their treatment in this introduction. It should be noted, however, that psychoanalytic theory and the knowledge derived from psychoanalytic treatment of neurotics have given us valuable help in the treatment of this type of delinquency as well as of those described.

EIGHT

THE AGGRESSIVE
GROUP

IN institutional work, grouping of the children is of primary importance. The therapeutic work of the institution for re-education will be the more effective the more the grouping itself is utilized to relieve the delinquency without respect to other educational measures. Although this conclusion may sound paradoxical, it is justified in actual practice. We know that "bad company" can influence a child toward delinquency, but it can be no more than a precipitating cause in a situation where the delinquency is latent. Community life in an institution is obviously unavoidable. The delinquent cannot be treated in isolation. To most people, it seems impossible that any good could result from forcing dissocial children to associate with each other in an institution. Parents often explain their unwillingness to put a child in an institution by saying, "What he does not already know, he will certainly learn there." Experience justifies this opinion; he does learn many things that he did not know before. The question remains, is it fantastic to think that group life can be effective in re-education? Proponents and critics of institutional treatment agree that a mutual influence within the group exists; they disagree as to how this influence operates. One school maintains that group life promotes delinquency: the other that it can be utilized to alleviate delinquency.

Is it not possible that both points of view have some justification and that the results depend on the circumstances under which the delinquents are brought together? The worker recognizes that depraved associates as a rule constitute a danger. However, he knows that this need not be true in the training school; on the contrary, he is convinced that grouping can be utilized advantageously if the groups are formed with proper discrimination. How these groups are formed, i. e., whether the worker should make the selection or whether the children should group themselves, is another question. If grouping were only a theoretical question, we should find it difficult to offer our critics adequate proof for our contention. Our conviction, however, grew out of our experience; it was forced upon us as we tried to explain to ourselves what actually took place in our institution. About this I shall now tell you.

At first we did not put great emphasis on the matter of grouping. It demanded our attention only in so far as we planned to have no more than twenty-five children in a group, to segregate the sexes, and to separate those of school age from the younger children. Otherwise, we allowed the children to remain together in the order in which they came to us. This created great difficulty for the staff, since every group contained some discontented members who blocked every effort of the worker. Corporal punishment or coercion was prohibited from the start. There followed a period of trial placement, of wandering from one group to another, until finally the groups were self-constituted. Thus we achieved a fairly homogeneous grouping. There remained, however, twelve boys who because of their behaviour difficulties were not tolerated in any group. Under the circumstances, we made a virtue of necessity and put the twelve together in a separate group which we shall term "the aggressive group."

These boys were our most troublesome cases. Almost unbelievable situations arose among them. At times fights arose in which they attacked each other with table knives and dishes. Even the stove was overturned in an attack. Their affect invariably took the form of outbreaks of rage. In this way, they showed a certain unity of psychological reactions. Our problem was to find the proper pedagogical attitude toward these children and the most effective manner of treating them. In the groups which had formed themselves, we continued our original policy of kindness without force. The aggressive group, however, aroused a great divergence of opinion on this point. In contrast to the self-formed groups, we had been forced by circumstances to bring these twelve arbitrarily together. Whether such an artificially constituted group could be held together without force was a question not to be lightly dismissed, especially since each member had created the greatest disturbance in his previous group. Many of our staff, among them our psychiatrist, contended that the most severe discipline and the hardest physical labour were necessary in handling these boys. I took the opposite point of view.

Later we shall discuss the significance of the pleasure-pain principle and take up more in detail the fact that a part of a child's adjustment to reality is not achieved if he has been treated with such severity that he develops an attitude of hate toward the people in his environment. In that phase of his ego development he remains a child. His aggression and hatred are only childish reactions resulting from the harshness which he experienced from the father or other persons in authority. If the educator employs even harsher discipline, he is using the same methods which brought the child into the original conflict. Thus he strengthens the antagonistic impulses which already existed and increases rather than mitigates the tendency to delinquency. The most effective procedure on the part of the educator is the direct opposite. At this time, I was not so certain of the correctness of my point of view because I had no real knowledge of the interplay of the psychic factors involved. I allowed myself to be guided by my intuition and only later became aware of the psychic determinants in the situation. Since the majority of the staff opposed my point of view, I took over the leadership of this group myself with two women workers who volunteered.

All we knew of the history of these boys was contained in the case history which was sent with each new admission. I have already told you that in our first contacts with a child we make it a rule to side with him in any discussion of the difficulties. We do this because it is of utmost importance to learn the boy's story from him, to understand his attitude toward life and how it is reflected in his behaviour. We therefore ask him questions and are not disturbed if he lies to us because that is only to be expected. What we learn from outside sources serves to confirm and expand our impression. We accept what the boy tells us of his actions as a natural response to a given situation. We must have all this information before we can undertake the task of clearing up his difficulties.

It was therefore important to have a personal interview with each one of the twelve boys. The group showed great physical variation. Some were small, weak, and undernourished; others were strong, robust, and developed beyond their chronological age. In no case was the home situation, as presented in the history, beyond reproach. Various family constellations were represented: dissension in the home, death of parents, separated parents, second marriages with step-parents, objectionable foster parents, adultery. All of this group showed retardation in school. Among the behaviour difficulties were truancy; stealing at school, at home, and from strangers; extremely aggressive behaviour at home, in school, and on the streets. The interviews not only confirmed the material in the histories but also added much that was new. In every case, there was a severe conflict between the two parents or with the child, so that the child was forced to take sides with either the father or the mother or against both. All these children had been brought up without affection and had suffered unreasonable severity and brutality. No one of them had had his need for affection satisfied; in some cases, love for a human being had been entirely transferred to an animal. They would speak with great tenderness of their pets only in the next moment to threaten their comrades with violence. All of these boys had been beaten unmercifully; they had hit back and had attacked when they felt that they were masters of the situation. In every case, a strong hate reaction was easily to be observed. It was evident that we were dealing with human beings who had been deprived of the affection necessary for their normal development.

This fact indicated the path our work must take. First we had to compensate for this great lack of love and then gradually and with great caution begin to make demands upon the children. Severity would have failed completely. Our treatment of this group could be characterized thus: a consistently friendly attitude, wholesome occupation, plenty of play to prevent aggression, and repeated talks with the individual members. No pressure that could be avoided was brought to bear on them. For instance, if a boy wanted to do something outside of the group activity of the moment, he was allowed to do so without question; or if he did not wish to eat at the table, he could take his food into the play room and sit in the corner; or if he did not like the play that was going on, he could break off. Of necessity there were regular hours for getting up, going to bed, meals, games, and so on. However, these were not binding on the individual. Our motto was: as far as possible, let the boys alone. The workers were to maintain their self-control however excessive the conduct became. They intervened in fights and brawls only to prevent injuries, without taking sides in the altercation.

Perhaps you will think that the children must have been very happy in this paradise where it was possible to live out their impulses without restraint, and that they showed their gratitude in good behaviour. This, however, was not the case. Their acts of aggression increased and took on greater intensity. This contradiction is understandable when we realize that before they came to us, they had suffered physical abuse and they therefore expected corporal punishment for any provocation. They could not grasp the new situation in any terms other than those of their past experience. Since they now encountered no brutal opposition, they could evaluate our attitude in only one way: "These workers are weaker than we are: they are afraid of us; therefore we can do as we please." These boys had never known kindliness. The only situations in which force had not been used against them were those in which they themselves had the upper hand. As a direct result of our attitude, their aggressive acts became more frequent and more violent until practically all the furniture in the building was destroyed, the window panes broken, the doors nearly kicked to pieces. It happened once that a boy sprang through a double window, ignoring his injuries from the broken glass. The dinner table was finally deserted because each one sought a corner in the play room where he crouched to devour his food. Screams and howls could be heard from afar. The building looked as if it harboured a

crowd of madmen. In spite of this, I continued to insist
that the boys be allowed to work out their aggression, that
there should be no intervention except when necessary to
prevent physical injury. The workers were required to be
absolutely impartial; they were to be equally pleasant to
all and to maintain their composure. In short, they were to
be a haven of peace in the midst of this chaos. The solution
of the problem of this group was due to the patient endur-
ance of these workers.

Another determinant of this behaviour which we shall
discuss later was their unconscious guilt feelings and need
for punishment. The cumulative aggression can be explained in still another way. The lack of affection in the
early environment had led them first to hate and later to
dissocial behaviour. A child tries to repay deprivation and
enforced pain by doing something that will bring pain
to another, and thus he achieves pleasure for himself. In
the institution, aggression which had proved effective in
the old environment did not bring forth the expected and
desired response. According to their earlier experience, any
other kind of response was inconceivable. When a boy
failed to achieve the desired reaction, it could only be because he was not aggressive enough. Therefore he must increase his aggression to such intensity that it would bring
about unconsciously wished for severity from the worker.
This severity had to be provoked in order to give him rational grounds for hating the worker. If he failed to secure
this response, he would no longer have any justification
for his whole attitude toward life.

It is easy to understand that aggression can rise only to a certain pitch. If we do not check its course, an explosion is inevitable. Since we did not oppose the destructive behaviour of this group, their aggression was bound to reach a climax. When this point came, the aggression changed its character. The outbreaks of rage against each other were no longer genuine, but were acted out for our benefit. I recall an incident of this period which had the appearance of being serious. One boy threatened another with a bread knife at his throat, yelling, "Cur, I'll cut your throat!" I stood by quietly, doing nothing and apparently taking no notice of the danger which seemed to threaten. It was clear that this was only a feigned attack and therefore not dangerous. Since I acted as if this were not unusual, our hero threw the knife on the floor in rage, stamped his feet furiously, and then let out an inarticulate howl which turned later into violent weeping and continued until he was exhausted and fell asleep. Similar scenes were enacted by each of the twelve. Our ignoring the aggression brought forth in each case violent emotion which spent itself in weeping with rage. These outbursts were followed by a period of emotional instability. At times, the boys were good, in fact, too good, and got along so well together that we enjoyed being with them. Then suddenly they would swing back to their old outbreaks, which increased our difficulties. However, these outbreaks gradually decreased in intensity. During this period, an emotional bond between the boys and the workers began to develop. Since we had become accustomed to their brutal emotional outbreaks, this

sudden change was disconcerting. The boys had become
unusually sensitive and now gave evidence of rivalry and
jealousy even greater in degree than that we expect to find
in the nursery. We had to proceed with caution. Our ex-
periment had now been going on more than three months,
and although the quiet periods were longer in duration,
we were apparently making no further progress.

We know what profound results affective experiences
can bring about. I am of the opinion that we shall be able
to shorten the period of institutional confinement when we
have learned how to create the proper emotional experiences
for the children and how to utilize them in retraining. As
yet we are too uncertain of these means and are afraid to
use them. Examples of this method we have seen in the
seventeen-year-old "man of the world," in the boy who stole
the money from the tobacco fund, and in the aggressive
group.

When this labile period had lasted for some weeks and we
seemed to be making no progress, I thought it a propitious
moment to heighten some strong pleasurable emotion. The
approaching Christmas festival offered an opportunity.
This group, like all the others, had its own Christmas tree
and special presents. It was a joy to observe what these
children experienced on that occasion. They talked about
it for weeks afterwards. A change had already taken place.
A few days after Christmas, we abandoned our demolished
quarters, the scene of our worst difficulties, to move into a
newly furnished building. In spite of the fact that the
other members of the staff disapproved of our giving these

incorrigibles another chance for destruction, we did not allow ourselves to be diverted from our plan. The twelve aggressives had developed into a homogeneous group which now presented no more difficulties than any other. At this time, I turned over the leadership of the group to our psychologist. He now had the difficult task of dealing with the boys through a period of extreme sensitivity, and of training and hardening them for the demands of real life outside the institution. This required discrimination and skill. He gradually increased the demands made on the boys. He was intentionally not always calm and friendly but showed his impatience and dissatisfaction; in short he exposed them to the influences they would meet in normal life. These formerly aggressive boys now became dependent charges. It is interesting to note that with the cessation of their aggressive behaviour, many of them showed superior mental performance and made up their lost school work.

The libidinal problem here involved warrants further study. We have endeavoured to explain the curative process. We conceive of this process as corresponding to that outlined in Freud's *Group Psychology and the Analysis of the Ego* [1] in that a strong emotional tie to the workers developed after the period of the greatest aggression. This intensive object relationship to the common leader paved the way for identification with him and in turn led to an emotional relationship to each other. Since no external pressure was exerted to hold them together, this tie was the

---

[1] Translated by James Strachey, International Psycho-Analytical Library, No. 6. London, 1922.

only force which held them together. Libido, no matter what its source, can be used as aggression that finds its expression in dissocial behaviour. How did this libido express itself after the change? Let us review the process. The workers did not allow themselves to oppose the boys; the boys responded to this with an increased feeling of their own power which found its expression in greater and more frequent acts of aggression; these later gave way to tears of rage, then to a period of sensitivity, and finally to acceptable behaviour. This discharge of affect through weeping was an abreaction which softened the aggression and lessened the sado-masochistic impulses against the leaders. The normal tender feeling which had been repressed found easier outlet after each discharge and, thus freed, was gradually able to attach itself to an appropriate object, the worker. When the transference was established, there followed an emotional relationship (identification) to their comrades, who were going through the same process. Thus we see the delinquent, who was previously isolated, gradually taking his place in a social group. The libidinal energy, freed through explosions of affect, could now be turned toward normal goals. We do not know if this sublimated libido would revert to its old channels if the boy were to return to his old environment. Our task was not merely to cure him but to make him immune before we sent him back to the former surroundings. To accomplish this, he should have been exposed to various group influences within the institution. This procedure, however, was impossible because it would have disturbed the other groups.

In evaluating our work, one should take into account the limitations under which it was carried on. The question arises whether better results could have been attained with a different procedure. If we could psychoanalyse a number of seemingly similar cases, we might arrive at some psychological insight which would enable us to formulate a valid theory of grouping. Only thus should we be able to form groups which would be effective for retraining.

We should note that one very important factor in the cure of dissocial children is their libidinal relationship to the worker. If the worker does not have the appropriate attitude toward the child, which he gains with psychoanalytic insight, even the most valuable method can come to naught. Unskilful handling of a situation by the worker can bring into play infantile libidinal attachments which are similar to those of the Œdipus complex, already known to you, and which, under certain circumstances, can lead to a rejection of the opposite sex.

I do not mean to give the impression that we made no mistakes in our work. It is difficult to avoid becoming emotionally involved oneself; this is a major problem in pedagogic relationships. Self-control requires a great deal of training. When two boys are having a fight, it is not easy to refrain from taking the part of the weaker, nor is it easy to keep one's temper when several boys stay in bed all morning. Another difficulty in our situation was that we had no assurance outside of our own intuitive feeling that we were in the right. We had set ourselves against majority opinion and were forced to carry on or admit defeat. This made it even harder for us to maintain our composure. I remember how happy we were after those long weeks of strain when the first peaceful week came, and then how downcast we were when things broke out again. Perhaps part of our success was due to our willingness to take a chance, our fearlessness, and also to the fact that we did not allow ourselves to be drawn into a guerrilla warfare. More important still, we were not afraid to let the boys grow up.

The difficulties in our work brought the members of the staff together for frequent conferences and created a close bond between the workers. Successful work of this sort is dependent on sympathetic co-operation of the staff. We learned a great deal from each other in our study of events as they took place. We often had occasion to recognize how unskilful handling in a given situation added fuel to the flame rather than letting it die down, and how intervention only brought more participants into an altercation.

The following is a detailed account of such an incident, in which half the aggressive group took active part and the others were drawn in occasionally. It began one afternoon at four and lasted until nine the next morning. This episode will show some of the difficulties of our work and the unfavourable influence of the mistakes of the worker on the course of events. The facts will be presented without interpretation.

The boys are in their quarters. One of the women workers is not well and is in bed; the other is on duty alone. The latter is serving the afternoon meal which consists of cocoa and one piece of bread for each boy. She gives each one the same amount of cocoa with a ladle from a kettle and a piece of bread from a basket which stands near her.

Four p.m. Louis, who has not responded when called to the meal but has gone on with his play, now comes to the bread basket and chooses the crusty end piece. The end piece was the favourite because it was the largest and so it was taken in turns. Its distribution was zealously guarded by the boys themselves. The worker failed to observe Louis's action as she had turned away. At this, the group becomes restless and calls the worker's attention to Louis! She speaks to Louis, who makes no response and goes into the room of the indisposed worker. The others finish their bread and cocoa and go back to their play. Only the helper for the week, Schultz, remains at the table. Each week one boy was chosen to be the worker's helper, a post of honour.

Four-twenty p.m. Louis returns in a very bad humour, which no one notices, and puts the end slice back into the basket. The worker had influenced him to do this against his will. With increasing bitterness, he drinks his cocoa, which has been left on the table for him, and then observes that the pitcher is empty and he cannot have his usual second helping.

Four-twenty-five p.m. At this, he becomes so irritated that he throws the ladle furiously into the pitcher, and when no one takes notice of him, he bangs his cup several times on the table.

Four-thirty p.m. He sees Schultz, the helper, eating his

end piece of bread and begins to annoy him, becoming more and more irritable. Since Schultz pays no attention and continues placidly to eat, Louis begins to scold.

Four-forty p.m. Louis hits Schultz with his fists, but stops when Schultz tries to defend himself. He picks up his cup and throws it at Schultz. Although Schultz is angry, he controls himself and makes no response.

Five p.m. The worker has succeeded in quieting Louis sufficiently so that he is now cutting kindling in a corner of the room. Rudy and Dan, special friends of Louis, have watched all this in the offing, and though they have taken no part, they are in a bad humour out of sympathy with their comrade. Rudy now shows his feeling by throwing the wood around the room and becomes even more annoyed when no one takes him to task for it. What he wishes to provoke is obvious as the sticks of wood fall nearer and nearer the worker.

Five-ten p.m. When the worker seems to be in danger and still shows no concern, George reprimands Rudy, but in a calm manner. Rudy is furious and stops throwing the wood because Louis attacks George. George refuses to let himself in for a fight and quietly leaves the room.

Five-fifteen p.m. Louis returns to his kindling; Rudy is still trembling with excitement and becomes defiant.

Five-thirty p.m. The worker clears up the cocoa cups. This was Rudy's task but in his resentment he has gone to the corner of the room and sat down by Louis without saying anything. In the meantime, some boys from another group have come to make a visit. These boys, together with

Willy of our group, feel it is disgraceful that the worker should have to do Rudy's work. One of the visitors remarks loud enough for Rudy to hear that in his group the worker never had to bother about the clearing up. Since Rudy takes no notice of this, the visitors and Willy say that Rudy ought to be ashamed of himself.

Five-forty p.m. Louis hears the reproach against his friend, leaves his kindling, and throws the speaker out of the room.

Five-fifty p.m. I come into the room to see what is going on because Schultz and George have come to me to report that Louis has thrown a visitor out. The worker had missed the two boys but did not know that they had gone to fetch me. The group is still upset. Dan is in an especially bad humour, Rudy is still defiant, and Louis, who has meanwhile carried the kindling into the worker's room, is still ready for a fight.

While I am talking with Louis, he has another outburst of emotion. Among other things he says, "I'd like to hear his bones crack." He means this for Willy, who scolded Rudy for not clearing up. During our talk together, some of Louis's emotion is drained off. In order to calm him completely, I propose that he go to my office with me to see some stereopticon pictures. He requests that his two friends, Rudy and Dan, be allowed to go, too. Besides these, two other boys join us.

Six-thirty p.m. I leave the building with the five boys. Louis, Rudy, and Dan, who were at first a little disagreeable, soon become friendly again. After we leave the group, it becomes apparent that two parties have developed from the events of the afternoon, and that one party has come with me.

Six-thirty-five p.m. The worker observes that George and Willy, who have been self-controlled during the afternoon, are now in a bad humour.

Six-forty p.m. Those who have remained behind go into the room of the indisposed worker to complain that they were not taken along. George, Willy, and Schultz accuse her of taking the part of the other boys, thus transferring to her their resentment against me. Willy stays angry for about half an hour and then cools off as suddenly as he became aroused. George and Schultz are merely vexed.

Seven-fifty p.m. After a long talk with the seven boys, the worker has succeeded in convincing them that they are wrong. George and Willy are so upset and touched because of the injustice done to the worker, that they begin to weep, but calm themselves quickly as she talks with them further.

Eight p.m. The opposing party returns from looking at the pictures. As Louis and his four companions enter the worker's room, they find the others sitting there peacefully, apparently in a good humour. This dampens their sense of victory, because they wish to triumph over the others who were left behind. Dan thereupon tries to tease the stay-at-homes, but is unsuccessful. The worker tries to influence them to give up the squabble and to be friendly with each other again.

Eight-twenty p.m. She achieves the opposite result. Louis considers that she is now with the other party, leaves her room in irritation, and sits down in the play room. Dan, also angry, and Rudy, who has fallen back into defiance, go with him.

Eight-thirty-five p.m. The rest go to bed. These three have meanwhile made a fire in the stove in the play room and they now announce that they are going to stay up all night. The worker can do nothing with them.

Nine p.m. The worker who was ill gets up. The three say that out of feeling for her, they will go to bed, but they demand that she stay with them until they fall asleep.

Nine a.m. Louis comes into the room of the worker on the pretext of getting his necktie fixed. He is weeping bitterly. The worker, surprised at this outbreak, goes to him and he announces spontaneously that he will not fight any more because he does not want to hurt her feelings. Louis is comforted and goes back beaming into the play room. When Rudy and Dan observe his good spirits, their mood, which had been labile all morning, becomes friendly and cheerful. By noon, the whole group is in a good humour again.

I have intentionally given you an example out of a time when our handling of our charges was still unskilful because I feel that you can derive more practical value for your work from our mistakes.

NINE

THE MEANING OF THE REALITY PRINCIPLE IN SOCIAL BEHAVIOUR

IN the first chapter, I introduced a problem for later discussion, saying that the child possesses inherent possibilities for adaptation to society and I expressed the opinion that education as well as experience has a distinct function to perform in the development of these potentialities. This is not a new theoretical assumption, but a fact which may be observed at any time, namely, that there is a constant interplay between experience and education.

Experience teaches us how to take care of ourselves; education has the further task of expanding this primitive adjustment to reality to such a point that we are capable of adaptation to the demands of society. Although we know that experience and education are inextricably interwoven in their effect on the child, let us assume a division in their work for the sake of our discussion. This enables us to make certain assumptions about education which will clarify one of the important aspects of remedial training. We must remember, however, that this division is only schematic.

Let us expand the conception outlined in the first chapter and assign to education the further work of preventing the development of anti-social potentialities. We can now turn our attention to those psychic processes which enable the small child to develop gradually from a being concerned almost exclusively with gratification of instinctual drives to one capable of taking his place in society.

Freud in his investigation of instincts [1] raised the question whether we can recognize the existence of a purpose in the functioning of our mental apparatus. He has found that this purpose is the attainment of pleasure. It appears to him that all mental activity aims at the securing of pleasure and the avoidance of pain. He explains how mental acts are regulated automatically by a tendency which he names the "pleasure principle."

When we hear about the pleasure principle for the first time, we are inclined to repudiate it, for we have learned from our own experience that the end result of a mental operation is often connected with pain. However, let us not be too hasty in our criticism but seek first to understand what Freud means. For this purpose we need only to follow his arguments. We have learned from him that the unconscious is the original source of all mental life and that instincts as well as wishes arise from the unconscious. Here the pleasure principle rules exclusively. What does this mean? Freud has observed that everything arising in the unconscious is directed toward the attainment of pleasure. The outer world, however, takes no cognizance of our need for pleasure, sometimes granting it, sometimes refusing it, according to the existing circumstances. In this way situa-

[1] *Introductory Lectures on Psycho-Analysis.*

tions often arise which do not correspond to the striving for pleasure but run directly counter to it. Let us take for example the infant who is still wholly dominated by unconscious functions. Its repose is disturbed by the imperious demands of physical needs arising from its instincts, which it strives to satisfy in order to avoid discomfort. It lives according to its instinctual demands, which are directed exclusively toward the attainment of pleasure and which ignore reality. Consequently the small child is subjected repeatedly to disappointments. The expected satisfaction is not achieved and pain instead of pleasure is experienced. At the same time, the child's psychic apparatus is undergoing changes that come with growth. The psychic apparatus is thereby forced to adapt itself to reality and, making the best of a poor bargain, it strives toward those adaptations which are the least dangerous to the personality. Naturally this adjustment is not achieved all at once. It is rather the result of a long process of development. From the unconscious, the ego receives information about physical functions, and through the sense organs about events in the outer world. Thus gradually it becomes capable of conforming to the demands of life. An important aspect of this development consists in a modification of the striving for pleasure. Pleasure may have to be postponed or renounced because of difficulties that stand in the way of instinctual gratification or because of the pain that may result from the gratification of instincts in a manner prohibited by society. This leads to the suppression of instinctual desires. The task of avoiding pain soon becomes as important as that of attaining pleasure. This renunciation of pleasure establishes a second principle which forces the conscious ego to regulate the unbridled pleasure impulses of the unconscious and to modify them in such a way that their satisfaction is harmless. This second tendency, which takes account of outer circumstances, Freud has named the "reality principle." The establishment of this principle means important progress in mental development. From this time on, the pleasure principle and the reality principle rule all mental processes: the reality principle in consciousness, the pleasure principle in the unconscious. While the pleasure ego seeks only pleasure and avoids pain, the reality ego strives for practical advantages and protects itself from harm. With an increase in the strength of the reality principle, the ego can defend itself better against instinctual demands. The earlier the individual recognizes the dangers which threaten him because of the contradiction between his instinctual desires and the demands of reality, the more capable he is of meeting reality.

When we understand these postulates of Freud, we see that the reality principle leads the growing child from his unreal world of pleasure into reality and enables him to make adjustments between his desire for pleasure and the demands of life. When the child is small and his capacity for adjustment to reality is still weak, the ego demands immediate instinctual satisfaction and is less able to forgo pleasure and to endure pain. We can define the different stages of the child's development according to the degree in which the pleasure principle predominates over the reality principle. Although the reality principle acts as a safeguard to the ego, it does not require the ego to renounce all pleasure. The reality principle, too, has pleasure as its goal, but it takes reality into consideration and contents itself with postponed pleasure or with a smaller degree of pleasure.

This explains the apparent contradiction that one can suffer pain while under the domination of the pleasure principle. Pain is endured under the reality principle in order to achieve more assured pleasure later. Pain may also arise from the encounter of an immature ego with reality; that is to say, the instinctual desires, regulated by the pleasure principle, break through prematurely in an individual not yet capable of dealing with them in relation to reality. Another possibility is that what is experienced in consciousness as pain may be experienced simultaneously as pleasure in the unconscious.

The educator must recognize clearly that the establishment and development of the reality principle result from the factors in the outer world which force the child to restrict his instinctual demands. However, we must not assume that the reality principle increases in strength in direct proportion to the amount of renunciation forced on the child. To assume this would be to disregard elements present in the child and to take only the outer factors into account. We must consider not only what the outer difficulties are but also how far these have been recognized and experienced by the child as such. Deprivations which are significant for one child may have no effect on another.

Each child reacts according to his own inherent tendencies.

What I have just said does not imply that we have such control over an individual child that we can arbitrarily regulate the deprivations he must endure in order to influence his adaptation to reality. Although we can influence these deprivations appreciably, it is dangerous to increase or decrease them beyond certain limits. In our discussion of the disturbances which lead to delinquency, we shall learn what happens when a child is subjected prematurely to extreme harshness or to extreme solicitude. How does a normally developed individual try to compensate himself for the pleasure denied him by reality? The ego does not submit without protest to the demands of reality when these demands are too great. Instead it takes refuge in a part of consciousness which is cut off from reality and which remains under the domination of the pleasure principle. I am sure you know to what mental process I refer. I mean fantasy, with which you are already acquainted. It begins in the child's play and continues later in day-dreams. If an individual is not contented with the meagre satisfactions which he can wrest from life, he enjoys in fantasy the freedom which he has long ago relinquished in reality.

We have intimated that experience and education have certain functions to perform in the development of the child's inherent potentialities. We have learned that the first adaptations to reality are biologically determined and that their expression is influenced by the circumstances in the outer world. This is the primitive adjustment to reality. Further development toward social adaptability is achieved through education. Thus the individual becomes capable of recognizing and submitting to the demands of society, and of co-operating in the maintenance and the advance of civilization. However, the ability to cope with reality and to further the work of civilization depends not only upon experience and education but also upon the individual himself. The capacity of the individual for adjustment to reality is determined less by the nature of the renunciations required of him than by the strength of the ego to meet them. In the same way, the capacity of an individual for education is determined chiefly by his constitutional endowment. In favourable cases the educator can so modify the environmental circumstances that they present the most advantageous conditions for development. The final result, however, depends on the child's ability to avail himself of the opportunities offered.

By social adaptation we mean the expansion of our first primitive adjustments to the stage of our present civilization. The educator of the child can only assist this developmental process, which the ego is forced to make in order to conform to reality. This aid consists in providing incentives for the conquest of the pleasure principle in favour of the reality principle. The long road mankind has travelled in attaining the present cultural level could not be traversed by the child in the short span of his growing up, without the help of education.

We now see what the incentives provided by education must do. Adaptation to reality involves renunciation. In order to bring about this adaptation the educator must proceed in conformity with life itself and erect dams that curb immediate instinctual gratification or make the gratification impossible. In this way he influences the child to suppress his instinctual demands, to postpone or renounce pleasure, and to endure pain. This method seems to contradict the present popular belief that the best education means letting the child do as he likes. Such a conception results either from confusing the means of education with its goal or from an attitude toward the problem which is coloured by our emotional experiences. It is incorrect to think that education means letting the child do as he pleases. Everyone who has had anything to do with little children knows that restraint and prohibition of momentary impulses belong to the order of the day and that the child must continually submit to limitations of his freedom. We ask ourselves: Is it true that the child has so many wishes that must be denied him? Could we not avoid prohibitions altogether? Let us imagine what a two-year-old child would do, if he met no hindrance. For example, he might pull the table cover off, break the dishes, climb up on the chairs and table without realizing he could fall and hurt himself. Is there anything a child would not try to put in his mouth, pry into, or break up if all his impulses were given free rein? How could we ever train him to be clean if we did not overcome his resistance to bodily care? We consider that these continual limitations of his freedom are in the child's interest, even though they seem to him violent attempts to hinder him in the satisfaction of his impulses. Naturally the child cannot renounce pleasure for reality without a struggle, but he must do this if he is to become socially acceptable. The educator will make this training as easy as possible and will at times offer no opposition because he understands that the little child is still dominated by the pleasure principle and that immediate pleasure is his most natural aim. However, he does this with the realization that such procedure is not education because it does not teach the child to renounce pleasure. How significant this freedom is for the child in later life, we shall learn in the next chapter, when we discuss the different levels in the ego.

A demand which leads to renunciation is effective only when it is recognized as such by the child, that is, when it corresponds to a similar wish in the child. The educator must choose between two possibilities in order to bring this about: either he allows the child to experience increased pain following forbidden instinctual satisfaction or he permits a substitute gratification. In both cases, he forces the child to renounce the desired pleasure. He accomplishes this either through punishment when the child will not give in or through recognition and love when he does give in. Thus the same end is attained by two diametrically opposed means, the fear of punishment and the reward of love. This fact has confused many people. To bring the child to renunciation through the reward of approval instead of through threats of punishment does not mean that we are indulging his desire for pleasure.

Generally speaking we have two methods of education. The one works with rewards, the other with punishment.

As a matter of fact, both methods obtain results. Some people become social because they fear punishment; others because they seek approval. Both methods, however, can result in failure as well as success.

If we were now concerned with the rearing of children and not with the *re-education* of *delinquents*, our present task would not be to decide which of these two methods we prefer, but rather to investigate in concrete cases which is the more advantageous.

Mistakes made in bringing up children interest us because of the part they may play in causing delinquency. We learned in the first chapter that all dissocial behaviour cannot be traced to poor upbringing. We shall consider later the fact that some unavoidable circumstances in life can produce situations the results of which may indicate that the child's training has been at fault.

It might be assumed that education will succeed in direct proportion to the love the child receives from his parents and educators. Within certain limits this is true. When these limits are exceeded, however, rewards as well as punishment not only lose their effectiveness, but even bring about results contrary to those desired. Let us not overlook the fact that rewards are useful only as stimuli or as means to achieve renunciation of pleasurable desires. If the parents bestow affection without asking any return by way of renunciation, the child does not need to exert himself. Assured of love, he lacks the incentive to give up pleasure in favour of reality. He thus retains the pleasure of direct instinctual gratification as well as the gratuitous love of his parents. A well-known example of this kind of training is the spoiled only child. He develops physically, but remains under the domination of the pleasure principle just as in his early childhood. This domination breaks down only when outer circumstances bring him unavoidable pain, or when the parents make an occasional demand on him in return for their love.

Let us now examine the second method of training in which indulgence in undesirable instinctual satisfactions is met with threat of punishment. If the child suffers too much from punishment or severity and is not compensated for this by the parents' love, he is forced into opposition and has no further incentive to submit to their demands and thus to subject himself to the reality principle. His main object is to resist authority. Rebellion against his parents, teachers, and society—the assertion of his ego against them—becomes just as great a source of pleasure to him as the gratification of his instincts. In this case, a counter-impulse may lead to persistence in childishness or, what is more likely, it may lead to a later rebellion which will destroy the effect of what had at first seemed successful training.

When either of these two methods of education goes astray, failure is inevitable. The over-powerful pleasure principle calls forth psychic reactions in undisciplined children that are different from those of normally developed children of the same age. Their behaviour makes them so conspicuous that we can easily see which of them need remedial training. We must help them when their undisciplined search for pleasure brings them into conflict with society. This thirst for pleasure we have long recognized as characteristic of the delinquent, and we have now found an explanation of this in the residue of childishness not yet given up.

The delinquent is like the child also in that he is not able to give up immediate pleasure in favour of later pleasure. He does and says things which are normal for an earlier stage of childhood development, but which make him appear abnormal and dissocial because they bring him into conflict with society. When we consider the various symptoms of delinquency in this light, they become understandable. In the training school as well as in the nursery there are incessant outbreaks of jealousy and constant quarrelling, not only among the younger children but also among the older ones. Most of them are like little children in regard to their physical care; uncombed hair and soiled clothes do not disturb them. A great many traits which the delinquents show can be interpreted as childish behaviour, even if greatly distorted. Like children, their interest span is short and their judgment is poor. They react immediately to any stimulus and give way to their feelings without restraint.

It seems as though only a part of the ego of the delinquent had succeeded in making the transition from the unconscious pleasure world of the small child to that of reality. Why have they remained immature in one part of their ego? Because another part of their ego has developed to a maturity corresponding to or exceeding their chrono-

logical age. Every delinquent shows this cleavage in the
ego. A part of the personality of the delinquent is dominated by the over-powerful pleasure principle; the remaining part of the personality may react in a reasonable and
mature way. The delinquent often shows himself especially
adept in conforming to reality in situations where the bare
struggle for existence is involved. One type of delinquent
shows under-developed sexuality. The others are normally
developed, or precocious. They are seldom perverse or in-
verted.

We now understand the delinquent as one disturbed in
his ego development. We recognize the origin of this disturbance, but as yet we do not understand how it arose. If
we draw an analogy to a neurosis, we arrive at a general
explanation. Two possibilities must be considered. In one
instance the phases of development have not run a normal
course because of faulty training; for instance, mental
functions or parts of them remain at an earlier developmental stage. This we designate as an "inhibition of
development." In the second instance, parts of mental
functions which had already reached a higher level of
development are for some reason pushed back to a lower
level. This we call "regression." In brief, we may say: Delinquency is the consequence of an inhibition of development or of a regression, which takes place somewhere along
the path from primitive reality adaptation to social adaptation. What is meant will be clearer when we compare the
delinquency which develops gradually with the delinquency
which breaks out suddenly in a previously normal indi-

vidual. We must remember that the delinquent is capable of primitive reality adaptation and that his difficulties arise in his progress from this point toward social conformity. His inability to assert himself in an acceptable manner brings him into conflict with society.

We shall examine more closely the two most striking types of delinquency, "delinquency caused by excess of love" and "delinquency caused by excess of severity," and I shall try to show you what remedial training must do in these cases.

The type "delinquent due to excess of love" is not often seen in the training school. However, he is found disproportionately often in middle-class homes and is the source of great sorrow and despair, though this is rarely admitted by the parents. These cases are frequently brought to the child-guidance clinic. I have seen many cases of "only children" in which the delinquency was caused by an excess of affection. We might assume that this indulgence results from a natural solicitude for an only child, or it may have other causes. For example, a woman who has lost her husband gives her whole love to the child, or divorced parents compete with each other in demonstrations of their love in order to win the child. More frequently, we find that the mother feels that she receives too little love from her husband. In some instances this feeling may be justified; in others it may arise from an excessive need for love which cannot be satisfied in a normal way. Occasionally we find a woman with an illegitimate daughter married to a man who is not the child's father. In these cases the stepfather often shows great devotion to his stepdaughter. When these marriages remain childless, the woman is usually inconsolable because she has borne her husband no children, and she cites as proof of her husband's desire for children his tender interest in the stepdaughter. She maintains that she spoils the daughter to please her husband.

This type of delinquency develops because the mother, or in some instances, the father, is not equal to the task of rearing the child. Mothers of this kind are well known to you and are not difficult to characterize. Since such a mother is ready to do anything to keep her darling from suffering the slightest discomfort, she is unable to subject him to any denials. Punishment upsets her more than it does the child. Weighed down by cares for him, she worries continually about his welfare and cannot demand from him any postponement or renunciation of pleasure. She clears out of his way all disappointments and obstacles which the child must learn to face and overcome in later life and thus she robs the child of initiative. His moods are endured with inexhaustible patience, and his naughtiness is admired as an indication of unusual individuality. Any criticism of him is as painful as a personal insult. The child's playmates are very severely criticized, especially if they offer resistance to his having his own way.

This child is the centre of interest and lives without restraint according to the wishes of his pleasure ego. Reality does not exist for him because his mother shuts it out. Since he is unable to modify the pleasure principle, reality is pushed further and further away. There are renunciations even for him, but they are always in the wrong place. His mother hinders him in his activity when there is any danger of bodily harm. He might fall down and hurt himself, he might take cold, he might upset his stomach, or get a headache! The child cannot understand these restrictions which stand in such contrast to his freedom in other respects, and he consequently rebels. But the mother lacks insight into this behaviour also. She tries to win his compliance with bribes of affection or with greater concessions in another direction. These methods soon lose their effectiveness, and the rebelliousness increases. Finally the child makes demands which the mother cannot meet. He can no longer be kept away from reality and when he has to meet it suddenly, he is unprepared for the force of its demands. This encounter either leads to neurosis or it kindles a rebellion which is beyond the control of the parents and which finds expression in all kinds of dissocial acts.

Delinquency of this type cannot be completely explained by the unconquered pleasure principle. We must also take into consideration libidinal relationships, which may not have been dealt with normally in earlier childhood. In our present discussion I shall disregard the latter factor as I wish to consider delinquency only from the point of view of the pleasure principle.

In the training school we find much more frequently the second type of delinquency: that which results from an excess of severity. We can recognize a third type also, in which the delinquency is the result of the practice of the two extremes of training at the same time, excess of severity and excess of affection. At first glance this may seem impossible, but it is easy to understand when we realize that two persons, mother and father, share in the child's training. Usually the father is too severe and the mother too indulgent.

Since childhood experiences are so significant for later life, we can understand the significance to the child of the normally strict father and the normally kind mother. The father usually represents the stern demands of reality and the mother softens these demands. This enables the child who develops normally to meet the later demands of reality with less pain.

When the father is too severe and the mother too indulgent, the mother will alter the father's demands not only in their form but also in their content, and thus the child escapes the father's demands through flight to the mother. When the mother makes certain demands in the interest of his physical protection which run counter to the pleasure principle, then the child can escape them through flight to the father. In this instance, the child conforms with the wishes of his father; but he suffers thereby no instinctual deprivation because he is acting in accord with the pleasure principle. Whether he turns to his father or to his mother, the child avoids reality, attains his pleasurable desires, and remains under the control of the pleasure principle. Thus he comes to rebel against both parents and finally becomes delinquent. The attitude of this type of delinquent can be epitomized thus: "Whatever I do, nothing can happen to me." This is clearly the result of the upbringing.

Such delinquency does not necessarily arise from actual experience of severity. Some children are as much affected by a quiet, cold attitude lacking in tenderness as others are by corporal punishment. We know that subjective reactions are decisive for the origin of delinquency. This must be kept in mind; otherwise we shall go astray in cases where the objective severity is lacking.

When a child is too strictly treated, or when through fate he experiences a crass encounter with reality too early, he is not able at this stage of his development to make the necessary adjustment to reality. A premature adaptation to reality is not accomplished, but as often happens, regression which takes the form of delinquency sets in after a period of apparently successful training. Thus the pleasure principle again achieves the mastery, as on the earlier level of development. We know from experience that when a child is thus forced back to an earlier developmental level to achieve satisfaction, he finds it more difficult to advance from this point than in the normal course of development. This child is progressively less amenable to force. The harshness of the child's training and life, which may have been borne patiently at one time, now lead to conscious opposition which often manifests itself in insubordination. This progresses to open rebellion, and in adolescents can lead to acts of violence.

All three of these types of delinquency could be studied from the point of view of infantile libidinal relations. Such a study would be instructive but it is outside our present task.

Remedial training has the same task in all three types. It must help the child to overcome the failures in his development so that he can exchange a childish level, where the pleasure principle predominates, for a level corresponding to his age, where the reality principle is effective. The educator must so guide the delinquent that he learns to exercise judgment; that is, the delinquent must develop the reality principle so that he is able before acting to decide between *immediate pleasure with later pain, and postponement or renunciation with later assured pleasure.* During the course of his training, the delinquent must learn that the amount of pleasure obtained from social conformity is greater than the sum of small pleasures derived from dissocial acts even when the accompanying discomfort of conformity is taken into account.

There is another important consideration which will enable us to avoid mistakes in judgment of dissocial behaviour. We do not have to find a neurotic factor in every case of delinquency. Sometimes the child's training is incomplete. The child's training may have failed to give him sufficiently strong incentives for the recognition of reality, or have made it possible for him to avoid unpleasantness, and thus the necessary development may have been interrupted or not made at all. We do not always have to assume that the unpleasant consequences of stealing give the delinquent unconscious pleasure, nor that every theft is due to unconscious guilt feelings. In many cases it seems probable that the delinquent is basically under the domination of a powerful pleasure principle and that, driven by his instincts, he automatically seeks satisfaction for his desires. *He is controlled by his pleasure ego; reality with its later unpleasant consequences does not exist for him at the moment.* Possibly this conception will arouse opposition. It is, however, the inevitable conclusion derived from observed facts, as well as from our theoretical considerations. We have by no means exhausted the question of the retraining of delinquents when we say that the problem consists in retrieving a neglected part of normal education. It is a far more complicated problem. To regard delinquency as the result of a failure in the child's upbringing is only one aspect of the problem.

A certain amount of instinctual deprivation is necessary for social adaptation. If this deprivation is too great or too little, the normal course of development does not follow. Thus it becomes the task of remedial training to make good this mistake.

Since we have decided that remedial training must help the child to a renunciation of his instinctual demands, it is not difficult to outline the procedure we must follow with the various types of delinquency in order to arouse the necessary incentives for renunciation.

The first and second types did not learn how to control their instincts because there was no need for them to do so; the third type failed because of their rebellion against restriction. These facts give us a point of attack.

The individual who was always certain of love at home, or who could turn from one parent to the other, must be held in the institution through a certain inner compulsion dependent on the sympathy and goodwill of the counsellor, which will spur him on to achievements and to the overcoming of his difficulties. This inner compulsion is not immediately established. It will be developed through the transference situation. Normally, however, it arises from the fact that the educator offers the reward of recognition only for some achievement on the part of the pupil.

The spoiled child who was allowed everything and who had all difficulties cleared out of his way defends himself against every outer force which demands the slightest deprivation, and refuses the simplest requests of the educator if they run counter to the wishes of his pleasure ego. This is not surprising or serious; it is the natural reaction to a new situation. If we did not endanger the results of our treatment we could wait until the transference is so positively established that the child is willing to forfeit direct pleasure because of his love for the counsellor. In this way, the domination of the pleasure principle is broken down rather than repressed. However, we cannot always wait for this process to take place. In the training school many insuperable difficulties arise which proceed from the pupil himself and from his parents. The pupil brought to the institution against his will has so many unpleasant experiences in the beginning that he can see no advantage in staying there. In this situation, he reacts just as he has at home; either he runs away from the institution or, more frequently, he writes to his parents urging them to take him away. In this letter he usually tells them about the abuse and discomforts which he must endure. He complains of the bad food, his failing health, and the cruelty of the teachers, and is full of promises of good behaviour if he is allowed to come home. As a last resort, he uses the most effective means to get what he wants: he threatens to kill himself if his parents do not come. The parents are alarmed and horrified over what they have done and they come in the greatest excitement to see whether their darling is alive or dead. When they find him living and far from emaciated, they overwhelm him with affection. They pour out their indignation on our heads, instead of on his. We cannot convince them of the unreasonableness of the boy's complaints because they themselves are not rational. It is especially difficult to make the mother see that her indulgence at home has caused the delinquency and that his gross exaggerations were meant to arouse their solicitude and force them to take him home. The parents remain incredulous and are convinced that their boy is not understood and that he is in an unsuitable environment. "There must be some truth in his statements," one hears continually. The parents cannot see that this is a natural reaction to the inevitable discomfort which must arise when a child is no longer allowed to realize his instinctual demands. The child triumphs, and he is taken home. Neither the child nor the parents realize that in a short time he will be as impossible at home as he was before.

The child whose delinquency is the result of too great severity at home comes from a *milieu* which, both subjectively and objectively, has offered him nothing but opposition to his desires. We must take an attitude toward him entirely different from that toward the delinquents described above. Here we must strive for a reconciliation with him; we must make good the love of which he has been deprived. Everything which we have said about the happy atmosphere of the institution is especially applicable to this boy. He needs the friendly, cheerful counsellor. He belongs in an environment where the adolescent's need for pleasure is satisfied. This environment must be so constituted that it gradually leads the child to an adjustment to the real world in which pain as well as pleasure exists.

Roughly expressed, each of these types of delinquent should find in the training school conditions exactly opposite to those of the former environment. The old style reformatory attempted through force, through fear of punishment, and without rewards of love to make the delinquent socially acceptable. Since most of their charges belong to the type just described, they only exaggerated what the parents had already begun and consequently they were doomed to failure.

That the modern training school uses another method is not especially praiseworthy. To the educator, this method is obvious because of the changed conception of the child's place in the family. It is correct as far as the type last described is concerned. However, this method is just as false for the first type as the old training-school methods were for the last.

I must emphasize that I am not presenting a theory of delinquency. I have done no more than to describe several striking features of delinquency and have discussed these from one point of view, which seems important for a first approach to the whole problem of delinquency.

The study of delinquency only from the pleasure principle is one-sided and not exhaustive. I have done this intentionally in order to offer you quite specific new insights. I shall present another aspect of delinquency in the next chapter.

TEN

SIGNIFICANCE OF THE EGO-IDEAL[1] IN SOCIAL BEHAVIOUR

IN the course of considering dissocial types, we have learned to recognize two phases of delinquency, the latent and the manifest. I have already mentioned one fact which is evident to all who deal with such cases, namely, that for the dissocial the conventions of society do not have the same effective force as for the socially adjusted. The variations shown in dissocial behaviour are only quantitative. The delinquency may go so far that accepted moral laws are completely ignored.

I have observed this not only in the consultation clinic but also in the institution. You caught a glimpse of it during your visit to the modern training school. We shall see more of it if we continue our inspection interrupted at that time. We need only note the pupils who have just arrived to make further observations. The "new" pupil is unmistakable.

Now let us visit the various groups and observe the new-

---

1 In this chapter, the terms "ego-ideal" and "super-ego" are used synonymously. Among the majority of writers in psychoanalysis, "super-ego" has gradually supplanted the older term, "ego-ideal." Recently there has been a tendency in psychoanalytic literature to use "ego-ideal" to differentiate special functions within the "super-ego."

comers. Their hands and faces are unwashed, their hair is uncombed and dishevelled, their shoes and clothing are dirty and torn. They keep to themselves, they seem depressed, or they laugh in an embarrassed way. Even in the midst of great bustle and confusion, their wild behaviour is striking. If we speak to them, they either stand silent and stubborn with their eyes on the ground, or laugh boldly in our faces or even turn their backs. From the worker in charge, we learn that they do not follow the routine; if they feel themselves misjudged they either react with open rebellion or store up their resentment for a subsequent outbreak. One child refuses to play when he is chosen; another refuses to play with certain children; a third plays only if he can be the leader and becomes stubborn and quarrelsome when this is not allowed. This obstinate and aggressive behaviour breaks up the unity of the group. The younger children are so hostile to school that they hide their books and supplies so that they cannot be found; the older ones in the workshop do the same with their tools. At mealtime they watch suspiciously to see if they are given the largest portion and are resentful if they feel any discrimination. Only crude, primitive things give them pleasure. They always enjoy a fight whether they take part in it, look on, or incite others. When they give a play, they "show off," hit each other in fun or maybe in earnest. The scenes depicted are fights, thievery, suicide, and murder. I could go further into detail about the characteristic behaviour of the "newcomer" but it is so apparent that even the unskilled eye observes it.

This behaviour of the newcomer calls forth all the severity of the personnel in the institution of the old type, but in the newer type is met with kindness and gentleness. *Must* we be content merely to use one method or the other, or can we come to a better understanding of these traits so typical of the dissocial individual? Perhaps we may reach some comprehension which will throw light on the whole problem of delinquency.

Let us try. We shall approach the problem with caution. We shall not push ahead too far at the outset but work in the hope of attaining some insight which will prove valuable for later use. We should first inquire why the majority of people submit without question to the demands of society before we can hope to understand what puts the delinquent outside social boundaries.

One thing is clear: the socially adjusted follow an inner voice which forbids a dissocial act, a categorical imperative which prescribes certain actions and compels other thoughts and impulses to be repressed. We feel certain that something in us observes what our active ego undertakes; it spurs the ego on or restrains it; is satisfied or dissatisfied with what the ego does; it praises, blames, or judges. For the present let us call this unknown faculty the critical ego, and let us compare it to a radio. Society broadcasts her demands over a certain wave-length. Our critical ego is the receiving apparatus; our active ego, the executive branch of a higher power, listens for directions and warnings. If the wave-length is incorrect, the receiving apparatus gives out false reports or none, and the listener hears false instructions or none at all. Thus left to his own devices, he is uncertain, stumbles, falls down, hurts himself, and goes into a rage.

But let us leave this comparison. The active ego is without a leader when its critical ego is not in agreement with the demands of society. In general, to be social means to have an ego which can subordinate itself to authority without conflict.

Having recognized this differentiation within the ego, the question necessarily arises why one individual can accept the social conventions and another cannot. This question must be put in another way and related to this differentiation in the ego. We are, therefore, interested in the critical ego and the active ego not only for themselves but because of their relation to each other.

Is the ego a product or function of the mind, of the soul, or of the body? Is it built up from two of these or from all three, and from what part of each?

This question cannot be answered adequately. It would be convenient if we could say something like this: In spite of the millions of tiny particles which go to make up our organism, in spite of the many varied processes in us, we have the consciousness of being not only an individual but a special individual, and this consciousness we derive from our ego. But this is only partly true; we cannot represent the ego as a unified organization existing entirely in consciousness, since Freud has discovered that many parts of the ego are unconscious.

For an explanation of the ego a deeper theoretical psychoanalytic preparation is necessary, which lies outside the scope of this book. I shall not attempt this but shall rely on your realization of your own personality, which enables you to conceive of your own ego although you have no exact representation for it, and I trust that many things will be clearer to you when we examine the way in which the ego is formed.

We have already suggested what the critical and the active ego are. For the present we shall not try to separate the ego into parts but consider it as a whole. After we have gone a little further we can take up the differentiation within the ego. That there is such a differentiation is not new to you because we have spoken in another chapter of the pleasure ego and the reality ego.

For the development of the ego, inner and outer determinants must be considered, that is, those arising within the individual and those approaching from the outer world. The reactions to these inner and outer stimuli leave definite impressions on the individual. We have already recognized this in the psychic development of the child. Let us recall what we have said about the emotional relationships of the small child, how the development of the infantile love life determines the form of the later love life. What we discussed at that time can serve as the basis for our present explanation. We know from Freud's researches that the infant, before he arrives at a realization of the world around him, uses his own body as a source of pleasure through the satisfaction of his organic needs. He does not require the outer world for the achievement of complete satisfaction. His own body, which stands at his disposal, quite suffices. In this lack of differentiation between his own ego and the environment, his ego, that is himself, is his world. From psychoanalysis, we know that infantile sexuality expresses itself autoerotically. I must again emphasize the fact that I use the word "sexuality" here in the broad psychoanalytic sense and that it must not be confused with genital sexuality.

After the autoerotic period, the child begins to notice individuals in the world around him. He gives them his attention, his interest, and his libido. We call this in dynamic terms "object cathexis" [cathexis in the sense of electric charge; German: *Besetzung*—Eds.] and mean that the child has suceeded in turning a part of his self-love toward objects in the outer world, and thus has changed "narcissistic libido" into "object libido." Freud has shown us the fate of such object cathexes which the child forms repeatedly in the course of his development and gives up in favour of new objects. This series of psychological changes does not fail to leave its trace on the child. Every object cathexis, that is, the attachment to a person, cannot be given up without leaving quite definite after-effects. What usually occurs? The child incorporates traits and characteristics of the loved person in his personality and thus preserves the love object in memory. When this process is complete, we call it "identification."

You may question whether an object must be given up before an identification can take place because we know from experience that the love for parents continues even after identification with them. Two comments can be made in regard to this. First, identification does not necessarily follow object love; they can be simultaneous. However, the identification with a given person will outlast the object love and, so to speak, preserve the memory. Second, the libidinal strivings proceed from the unconscious, attach themselves to an object in the outer world, and are thereby satisfied. In an advanced identification, the ego takes over so much from the love object that it can finally present itself to the unconscious as a love object and what seems to be object love is often only self-love. Thus object libido is reconverted into narcissistic libido. It is possible that identification can take place without previous object cathexis. Freud has found that the small boy goes through a phase of direct identification with the father before he establishes his first object cathexis. He calls this the primary identification, which receives reinforcement through the later identifications. This explains the special place of the father in the life of the individual and society.

I must warn you against a misunderstanding. The giving up of an object cathexis does not always mean hating the object which was formerly loved. We saw in Chapter Four, in the case of the boy who was aggressive against his sister, that this hate was the result not only of an incestuous tie to her but also of an object cathexis which had not undergone a normal resolution. In the case of this boy, it was a question of repression; but in our present discussion, we are concerned with the real giving up of the object.

Since new traits are incorporated into a child's personality through identification every time he gives up a love object, it is easy to understand why children continually change in the growing-up process. We understand also what Freud means when he says that the character of an individual is the precipitate of relinquished object cathexes and comprises the history of these object choices. But we must not think of these new traits as being laid down one upon the other. How the child builds these traits into his personality depends on how he reacts to the influences of these love objects, how he assimilates these influences or defends himself against them.

The amount of change which takes place in the child's ego depends on his age at the time of the identification. We can easily conceive that the identification is the more effective the earlier it takes place. Therefore, to understand the structure of the ego, we must take into consideration not only constitutional and environmental factors, but also object cathexes with their consequent identifications and the age periods in which they took place. The first identifications have the most lasting effect because they are the most sharply imprinted on the still weak and dependent ego. The first objects in the outer world are the parents and the nurse. In a normal situation, it is the parents with whom the most important identifications take place.

We have followed in several instances the fate of the libidinal strivings toward the parents; in the second chapter with the boy who went to the country to get cherries for his mother, and in the third chapter with the boy who experienced the trauma of the terrible death of his mother.

At this point we took up for the first time the Œdipus complex and discussed what was pertinent to that case. We saw there that in the course of a child's development traits of both parents are incorporated into his being.

Now we can discuss this more in detail and go more deeply into the Œdipus complex. Its fate is sealed if the child develops normally. It dominates the first period of the child's libidinal development. This period of infantile sexuality is normally succeeded by a second period in which sexual strivings are quiescent. This we call the latency period.

When the Œdipus complex comes to an end, the object cathexes concerned are given up and are replaced, as you have already heard, by an identification with the father and the mother. At this point the two opposing trends of the Œdipus complex, that is, the positive and the negative, in some way combine.

Freud has also found that a definite result is brought about through the demands made upon the child by the Œdipus situation and by the identifications which take place in this very early period of the child's life. What is this result? These identifications as well as those that follow not only bring about changes in the ego but they take a special position within it. This corresponds to the earlier position of the father and the mother in the outer world. This part of the ego sets itself up against the remaining part as a critical faculty, taking a role similar to that which the parents formerly played. Freud designates this part of the ego the "super-ego," or "ego-ideal."

We can picture to ourselves the development of this ego-ideal thus: Father and mother are loved; they allow and permit. Both are recognized as persons in authority, especially the father. They are real and present, and force the child to limit his instinctual satisfactions through affection or through fear. The father not only checks the libidinal strivings of the boy toward the mother, thus diverting them into another channel, but he also makes his authority felt through commands and prohibitions which mean renunciation on the part of the child. He gives commands which must be fulfilled. "You *ought to be* such and such (like your father); it also comprises the prohibition: You *must not be* such and such (like your father); that is, you may not do all that he does; many things are his prerogative." [2] His desire to be like the father makes him want to grow up. The father, who represents to the child the demands of society, forces him to fulfil these demands through the child's identification with him. This is only possible when instinctual gratification is renounced and the instinctual drive is diverted from its original primitive goal to a higher one, i. e., when a higher cultural level is attained. Thus the father with his demands for renunciation provides the initial impulse toward the higher development of the psyche. The influence of the parental demands and of those parental traits that seemed to the child worthy of emulation continues operative even after identification has taken place, and eventually assumes the character of

[2] *The Ego and the Id,* by Sigmund Freud, M.D., LL.D.; English translation by Joan Riviere; pp. 44–5. London, Hogarth, 1927.

imperative command. Thus the super-ego takes its form and content from identifications which result from the child's effort to emulate the parent. It is evolved not only because the parent loves the child, but also because the child fears the parent's demands.

In its peculiar position, the ego-ideal has the ability to dominate the ego. "It is a memorial of the former weakness and dependence of the ego, and the mature ego remains subject to its domination. As the child was once compelled to obey its parents, so the ego submits to the categorical imperative pronounced by its super-ego." [3] "The more intense the Œdipus complex was and the more rapidly it succumbed to repression (under the influence of discipline, religious teaching, schooling, and reading) the more exacting later on is the domination of the super-ego over the ego." [4] When we read in psychoanalytic literature that the development of the child in his main traits is already determined by the fifth or sixth year, we must not misunderstand and construe that to mean that the child is not capable of education after that time. This means only that these early impressions, received by the child from his parents, have a permanent effect on the formation of his character. The super-ego receives important contributions in the further course of the child's development from teachers, heroes of literature, and persons in authority who continue the role of father. Many people could not hold their own in life if their ego-ideal were derived solely from the parents.

[3] *Op. cit.*, p. 69.
[4] *Ibid.*, p. 45.

The ego-ideal is "the representation of our relation to our parents. When we were little children we knew these higher natures, we admired them and feared them; and later we took them into ourselves." [5]

We have now learned that the ego-ideal consists of that part of the ego which sits in judgment over the rest of the ego. We do not need to search for words to describe the ego-ideal as a moral censor. We have long been acquainted with this inner voice and have called it conscience.

I repeat, "The ego-ideal owes its special position in the ego or in regard to the ego to a factor which must be considered from two sides: to the fact that on the one hand it was the first identification, and one which took place while the ego was still feeble, and that on the other hand it was the heir to the Œdipus complex and thus incorporated into the ego objects of far greater significance than any others." [6] It is not rigid and unchangeable, but accessible to later influences and keeps the ability taken over from the father to oppose, to guide, and to dominate the ego. We must note that the demands of society are presented to the child through the father's attitudes and activities, and that the child therefore receives his social orientation from the father. Thus the ego-ideal takes on features which exclude the possibility of later unsocial conduct.

There is another automatic process most important for the communal life of man which I must call to your attention. In families with several children, in schools, etc., it

---

[5] *Op. cit.,* pp. 46–7.
[6] *Op. cit.,* pp. 68–9.

happens necessarily that several children take over the same traits that occur in the father, the teacher, or the person in authority. The more similar these traits the less variation we shall find in the ego-ideal of the children. The relationship that children bear to each other determines the traits they adopt and those they reject. However, certain traits are generally adopted: understanding, generosity, sociability, orderliness, conformity to social demands, and restrictions of the satisfaction of instincts. What we call social feeling is necessary for development. One may say in general, "Social feelings rest on the foundation of identifications with others, on the basis of an ego-ideal in common with them." [7]

We have thus roughly outlined the question we put at the beginning, how do we become social, and we must now turn to the delinquent, that is, to those whom the environment so designates. It is not difficult to see what direction our study must take. The difference between the delinquent and other people is a question of the ego-ideal, the ego, and the relation of these to each other.

What you have heard of the ego and the ego-ideal concerned itself with the normal development of both, so that an ego-ideal whose demands are reasonable is found associated with a similarly constituted ego whose demands the ego-ideal can accept and fulfil. This, however, is not always the case. We shall have accounted for many expressions of delinquency when we recognize that either the ego-ideal may lack some of the qualities which society demands

---

[7] *Op. cit.*, p. 49.

or that the ego-ideal may take up socially acceptable demands in a distorted way or not at all. A child needs only to grow up in a dissocial environment, to identify himself with dissocial or criminal parents, in order to develop an ego-ideal which is unacceptable to society. This is the same mechanism that operates to keep the adjusted individual in social equilibrium. In cases of delinquency, the ego and the ego-ideal are normal in their relation to each other, but their attitude to the outside world deviates from the accepted standards. This we see illustrated in the formation of dissocial or criminal gangs. Within these groups the individuals are completely social.

The extreme cases in these groups are often incorrectly designated as "born" criminals. One speaks of families of criminals, or even generations of criminals, and means thereby that the criminal constitution, about which we have only vague ideas, is inherited. This may be true, but the worker who is concerned with dissocial types does not exclude other possibilities even though he is told that the father and grandfather of his charge were criminals. He recognizes the process of object cathexis and identification, the driving power of traits taken over from the parents into the ego-ideal, which forces the individual to do what, as a child, he saw his father do. Thus, a generation of criminals can arise without any constitutional criminal inheritance.

It cannot be denied that sometimes a faulty ego-ideal is developed on the basis of hereditarily determined structural deficiencies, and delinquency results. To put it in another way, there are dissocial types with inborn defects, who lack the inherited capacity for object cathexis and identification. Whether this is a quantitative or a qualitative lack, whether object cathexis or identification or both do not function properly, is a problem for investigation. It is questionable, however, whether the constitutional lack can be so great that we can assume the individual was criminal from birth. In these cases of constitutionally determined dissocial behaviour, we can accomplish nothing because educational means do not help us. We must classify these cases as incapable of social adaptation and thereby excluded from the possibilities of social retraining.

Even when the psychic apparatus of the child is normal and the mechanism for object cathexis and identification functions properly, the formation of a normal socially acceptable ego-ideal is still not guaranteed. We have spoken of the normal ego-ideal which goes astray because it takes over unacceptable traits from the parents. There are many other external circumstances which make the formation of a socially acceptable ego-ideal difficult, or even impossible. I cite a few cases to illustrate what I mean.

The father is a brutal man who brooks no opposition. Everyone must give in to him. The mother and children fear this tyrant who does not shrink from beating the whole family, including the mother.

Or the converse: The father is a weakling, inconsistent in his discipline, unstable, controlled by momentary impulses, the plaything of his own unconscious drives and of outer circumstances.

Or another: The father is a drunkard, and under the influence of liquor behaves outrageously in the home, even forcing sexual intercourse on his wife before the children, and goes into such rages that he destroys the furniture and forces the family to flee to the neighbours for protection.

Still another case: The child grows up in the midst of a conflict between the parents. The father is one of the types pictured above, the mother is a nagging, quarrelsome, abusive woman, an aggressive masculine type, and continual fighting goes on between the pair.

Finally, the following constellation: Divorced or separated parents play the child against each other.

You will recall from your own experience similar or worse family situations in which delinquency can be explained through identification with the parents.

The formation of a socially directed ego-ideal cannot take place if the nucleus of the ego-ideal, which, as you know, is based on the first great love objects, is weak or non-existent. Furthermore, object cathexis and identification require time to establish themselves. Let us take, for example, an illegitimate child or one who has lost his parents early in life or who comes unwanted into the world or who wanders from one foster home to another. Before he can form a real object relationship or make a proper identification, he is already on his way to a new environment, to new people. The development of these mechanisms is thus continually interrupted and cannot be brought to fulfilment. These beginnings of character formation have no stability, but remain a weak intimation of what might take place and do not prove strong enough to give direction to the later life. If to this is added unkind treatment in the various foster homes, we can expect a still weaker ego-ideal.

Let us take another case: An illegitimate child or a child whose father is dead lives alone with the mother. There is no man to take his place and the mother is an easygoing, indulgent woman. The ego-ideal of this growing boy will lack the characteristics which later form the categorical imperative in relation to the ego, unless he acquires these later through identification with someone who takes over the father role.

From these facts, the worker in this field should draw some conclusions for his own procedure. He must secure detailed information concerning the early life of the child. He should not be content with finding out when the child was born, at what age he began to talk and walk, whether he had convulsions or not, etc. It is of the greatest interest to him to find out about the child's earliest libidinal relationships. It is important to know about the various foster homes in which the child may have lived, the length of stay in each, how he was treated, to whom he showed an especial inclination, against whom he was most aggressive.

I have given you a cursory account of the many possibilities which can influence the ego-ideal unfavourably and lead to delinquency. Another type of ego-ideal formation should be mentioned. It arises when the mechanisms of object cathexis and identification are played against each other instead of developing harmoniously. It is difficult to

picture such a dynamic process because these mechanisms,
as they appear in dissocial types, have not yet been closely
studied. We must be satisfied for the present to set it down
schematically: The object cathexes arise in the unconscious
and establish themselves at first without any influence from
the conscious personality. If a resistance arises in the ego
against the cathexis, it disturbs the identification and
finally operates as a lack or defect in the ego-ideal. For
example, in the family with the brutal father, mentioned
above, the mother and father are both love objects for the
child. Through his identification with the mother, the child
can experience the father's brutal treatment as so unpleasant that an aggressive impulse against the father will be
freed. This will naturally influence the character of the
identification with the father so that the ego-ideal is no
longer normal in its relation to the ego. This can make the
child dissocial.

The interdependent inner and outer factors, which make
disturbance in the formation of the ego-ideal possible, can
occur and operate in various forms and in differing and
variable combinations. In every case of dissocial behaviour,
these factors show both quantitative and qualitative differences. Thus we can explain some of the finer individual
variations within the dissocial types. Here is still another
unexplored field for an intensive study through psychoanalysis of the deeper relationships existing between the
psychic processes.

Let us consider a case where the ego attempts to withdraw itself from the demands of the ego-ideal. The ego-

ideal demands too much. The ego is too weak to meet these demands or it defends itself against them. Does the ego-ideal remain silent, does it acquiesce, or how does it behave? It is not silent; its moral censor, the conscience, threatens it and forces it to submit. Even if the ego is stubborn and insistent, the ego-ideal does not give up the struggle and releases in the ego what we term feelings of guilt. In order to understand the further course of the conflict between the two we must take up the psychic processes in question.

We know already that the ego-ideal criticizes the activities of the ego and judges its thoughts and impulses. The criticism of the ego-ideal would have no meaning if it did not succeed in forcing itself into the perception of the ego. If there is no contradiction between what the ego-ideal dictates and what the ego carries out, thinks, or feels as an impulse, if the ego and the ego-ideal are agreed, then no conflict arises. But it is otherwise when the ego-ideal sits in judgment on the ego. This is perceived in the ego as a feeling of guilt. It is easy to understand that the ego thus falls into a conflict, the severity of which varies with the insistence of the demands of the ego-ideal for the fulfilment of its claims. The more the conscience warns and threatens, the more painful are the guilt feelings which emerge into consciousness. The conflict would be over at once if the ego gave in to the demands of the ego-ideal. This of course does happen repeatedly but it does not concern our present discussion. We must find out what happens when the ego wishes to withdraw from the demands of the ego-ideal. It has at its disposal a defence mechanism which is

already known to you in another connexion. If the guilt
feeling becomes unbearable, the ego defends itself against
it just as it does against all other things which are unacceptable in consciousness; that is, the guilt feeling is repressed and becomes unconscious. "We know that as a rule
the ego carries out repressions in the service and at the
behest of its super-ego; but this is a case in which it has
turned the same weapon against its harsh taskmaster." [8]

Like all the other material withheld from the control of
consciousness, whether it has been forced back into the unconscious or whether as originally unconscious material it
has never been dealt with, the sense of guilt grows luxuri-
antly. The ego is not freed from the feeling of guilt even
after it has pushed this back into the unconscious. This can
give rise to mental illness, to delinquency and, through the
cumulation of the "unconscious sense of guilt," to crim-
inality. The mental illnesses which can thus arise do not belong to our discussion. The worker in our field is interested
in dissocial and delinquent children and youth. He wants
to know if and how one can recognize dissocial behaviour
derived from an unconscious sense of guilt. In general, we
can say that unconscious guilt feeling motivates dissocial
behaviour more often than is realized. The worker trained
in psychoanalysis will not fail to recognize the unconscious
need for punishment which goes hand in hand with this
feeling of guilt.

Let us consider a few cases by way of example.

You remember the story of the girl who stole the under-

---

[8] *Op. cit.*, p. 75.

wear out of the chest while her mother was dying. She used the money to have a good time in an amusement park. In the institution she was rebellious and insubordinate and troubled with anxiety dreams. Here we have a case in which the dissocial behaviour arose out of unconscious guilt feeling or need for punishment. Let us recall the aggressive cases in our institution who did everything they could to provoke punishment. The unconscious sense of guilt prevents acceptance of kindness from the teacher and invites corporal punishment. This girl and the aggressive boys behaved in a way which, according to their previous experience in life, was calculated to provoke punishment.

Another case: A youth steals some money at home and buys himself a cap. Although he knows that the cap will certainly attract attention, he comes home with it on his head. In this case, we can assume the presence of an unconscious feeling of guilt.

The same is true of the boy who wrote down his sins on a piece of paper so that he could not forget to confess them. Among his sins, he listed a theft of money from his father, then he placed the paper in his report-book (which was extremely good) so that his father found it when he had to sign the report card. For this boy the atonement imposed in the confessional was not sufficient.

When children take money only to give it away, as is often the case, the unconscious sense of guilt may also be operative. In the same way, criminals who carry out their crimes in an awkward way in order to get caught, or those who go back to the scene of the crime in spite of the risk involved, are motivated by their unconscious desire for punishment.

Perhaps these conceptions are difficult for you to grasp and accept, but after you have dealt with dissocial types, you cannot fail to recognize the domination of these unconscious guilt feelings against which the delinquent is powerless. Freud has called our attention to the fact "that in many criminals, especially youthful ones, it is possible to detect a very powerful sense of guilt which existed before the crime and is not therefore the result of it but its motive. It is as if it had been a relief to be able to fasten this unconscious sense of guilt onto something real and immediate." [9]

The delinquents of this type are the victims of their own morality. They try to withdraw themselves from the too severe demands of their ego-ideal and are punished for so doing. But we do not need to turn to delinquents to observe the operation of unconscious guilt feeling. Much naughtiness in the nursery and misbehaviour in school can be attributed to the same mechanism. We fall in with these children's demands when we punish them. Their need for punishment is satisfied for the moment and no change in their behaviour is achieved. This unconscious guilt feeling can attach itself to an actual deed and the punishment which follows produces pleasure instead of pain, gives temporary relief and allows the child to remain rebellious or hostile to discipline. Ordinary methods of education do not suffice in such cases. Without bringing to light the

---

[9] *Op. cit.,* p. 76.

unconscious guilt, we can accomplish nothing educationally either with normal or dissocial children.

The unconscious feelings of guilt which form the basis
of these cases of delinquency may never have been conscious. These feelings in part may remain unconscious
from the beginning since the origin of the unconscious
guilt feeling is closely bound up with the Œdipus complex, which also remains unconscious. These difficult matters must remain outside the realm of the remedial educator because he will not know how to deal with the factors
which determine the delinquency. *This* is the task of the
psychoanalyst. We can close this part of our discussion
with the recognition that many delinquencies arise from
the desire of an individual to relieve himself of the severe
demands of his ego-ideal, whereby unconscious feelings of
guilt become the motivating force behind the delinquency.

Changes in the attitude of the ego toward the ego-ideal
can occur also as a result of psychic illness. Freud has
shown us that those psychic disturbances which occur in
the relationship of the ego to the outer world can occur also
between the ego and the ego-ideal. I shall not take up
these illnesses nor the types of delinquency arising from
these sources. To do this would involve a far greater discussion of psychoanalysis than is permissible in this book.

When we consider the above discussion, we find that the
question, whether the dissocial should be treated with severity, as in the old style institution, or with gentleness, as
in the modern one, does not meet the real problem at all.
These two methods arise out of opposed emotional attitudes

to the delinquent and do not take into consideration the fact that one type can be influenced and made socially acceptable through severity, another through gentleness, and that a third responds to neither one of these methods; and that the usual educational methods are in general ineffective. Why is this?

Socially acceptable behaviour is preserved by means of the ego-ideal, which frees normal conscious feelings of guilt. With the delinquent this does not obtain. These feelings are either repressed, weak, or non-existent. If the ego-ideal is excessively severe, as in the border-line neurotic cases with dissocial features, the worker achieves therapeutic results through being kind and gentle and reducing his demands on the child. If the delinquent is an uninhibited primitive type who has not learned to adjust himself to reality because the restrictions placed on his instincts were too slight, the worker must begin with increased demands. Thus every type of delinquency requires a special type of treatment. In all cases, however, the treatment must concern itself with the further development of the ego-ideal, and we must put the question thus: how can we direct social retraining in order to bring about corrections of character in the individual?

I cannot close this book without once more stressing the great importance of the personality of the workers in this field. You have seen that a character change in the delinquent means a change in his ego-ideal. This occurs when new traits are taken over by the individual. The source of these traits is the worker himself. He is the important object with whom the dissocial child or youth can retrieve the defective or non-existent identification and with whom he can experience all the things in which his father failed him. With the worker's help, the youth acquires the necessary feeling relation to his companions which enables him to overcome the dissocial traits. The word "father-substitute," so often used in connexion with remedial education, receives its rightful connotation in this conception of the task.

What helps the worker most in therapy with the dissocial? The transference! And especially what we recognize as the positive transference. It is above all the tender feeling for the teacher that gives the pupil the incentive to do what is prescribed and not to do what is forbidden. The teacher, as a libidinally charged object for the pupil, offers traits for identification that bring about a lasting change in the structure of the ego-ideal. This in turn effects a change in the behaviour of the formerly dissocial child. We cannot imagine a person who is unsocial as a worker in this field. We assume therefore that the ego-ideal of the child will be corrected through the worker's help in bringing him to a recognition of the claims of society and to participation in society. Our work differs from that of the psychoanalyst in that we use the transference to accomplish an entirely different task. In the analysis of neurotic patients, the transference must be used, not for temporary improvement, but to give the patient strength to complete a special piece of work, to change unconscious material into conscious material and thereby to bring about a permanent change in his whole being. In remedial training we cannot be content with transient results which arise from the emotional tie of the dissocial boy or girl to the worker. We must succeed, as in psychoanalysis, in bringing the wayward youth under the influence of the transference to a definite achievement. This achievement consists in a real character change, in the setting up of a socially directed ego-ideal, that is, in the retrieving of that part of his development which is necessary for a proper adjustment to society.